THINGS BETWEEN US

ONE-ACT PLAYS
BY JACQUELYN REINGOLD

★

★

DRAMATISTS
PLAY SERVICE
INC.

ACKNOWLEDGMENTS

Many thanks to the theatres that produced and developed these plays: HB Playwrights Theatre, Ensemble Studio Theatre, Naked Angels, MCC Theatre, New Dramatists; the many actors and directors who worked their magic on them; the people who inspired them: Rich, Scott, Nancy, Kurt, Alex; Glenn Young for publishing four in *Best American Short Plays*; to John for the title; and to Stephen Sultan and Scott Yoselow, for making this happen.

AUTHOR'S NOTE

While these plays were written separately, without the idea of performing them together, they can be presented as a complete evening. Done that way there should be an intermission after 2B (OR NOT 2B), and I suggest you leave out DEAR KENNETH BLAKE, which perhaps doesn't fit with the tone of the others, and one other, in the interest of brevity.

CONTENTS

JOE AND STEW'S THEATRE OF BROTHERLY LOVE AND FINANCIAL SUCCESS

JOE AND STEW'S THEATRE OF BROTHERLY LOVE AND FINANCIAL SUCCESS was first produced by the All Seasons Theatre (John McCormack, Artistic Director) in New York City in 2000. It was directed by Warren Leight. The cast was as follows:

STEW .... Ean Sheehy
JOE .... Greg Esposito

CHARACTERS

STEW, a cockroach. Smart and sensitive.

JOE, his brother. Also a cockroach. Not so smart and not so sensitive.

THE CRITIC, a human. Sort of. Offstage.

PLACE

An Off-Off-Broadway theatre.

TIME

Any minute.

NOTE: Theatre and play references/jokes should be adapted/updated to fit place/time.

JOE AND STEW'S THEATRE OF BROTHERLY LOVE AND FINANCIAL SUCCESS

The sound of a loud explosion. Lights up. Debris is everywhere. We hear voices from under a pile.

STEW. Whoa! What was that?
JOE. I don't know.
STEW. You OK? Joe?
JOE. I don't know. You?
STEW. I don't know. Where are you?
JOE. I don't know.
STEW. Can you see?
JOE. Not really.
STEW. Me either. That was pretty bright.
JOE. Yeah.
STEW. And loud.
JOE. No kidding.
STEW. That wasn't in last night. Must be new, huh?
JOE. I guess.
STEW. I don't see how it makes sense.
JOE. Didn't make no sense to me.
STEW. I mean dramatically, you know. *(Stew emerges from the pile. He is a cockroach. He looks around at the mess.)* Wow. *(To himself.)* Very realistic. Very site specific. Very breaking the fourth wall.
JOE. What?
STEW. Nothing.
JOE. Ow! Damn.
STEW. You OK?
JOE. Yo, I don't know, I'm stuck. I'm under a beam or somethin'.
STEW. OK, I'm coming, I'm coming. Just keep talking.
JOE. Three of my damn legs are stuck under a damn two-by-four

and it's cutting off my Goddamn circulation! *(Stew removes a broomstick [toothpick] from Joe's legs. He emerges. He is a cockroach, too.)* What was that thing?
STEW. Toothpick. You OK?
JOE. Yeah. I think so.
STEW. Antenna?
JOE. *(He checks.)* Fine.
STEW. Legs?
JOE. All there.
STEW. Carapace?
JOE. In one piece.
STEW. That was close.
JOE. Sure was. Hey, you saved my life, Stew.
STEW. Ah, what are brothers for? *(They clap each other on the back.)*
JOE. *(Notices the surroundings.)* Wow. What a mess.
STEW. Impressive, huh?
JOE. Uh oh.
STEW. What?
JOE. Where are those brownie crumbs?! I worked all week to collect them. *(He searches.)*
STEW. Uh oh.
JOE. What?
STEW. What do you hear?
JOE. Nothing.
STEW. This is the part in Act Two where they yell and have that big fight. "You son of a bitch!" "You daughter of a bitch!" Remember?
JOE. Not really.
STEW. We better go look.
JOE. I'll stay here. *(They look at the audience.)*
STEW. The actors — they're — gone.
JOE. Human toast.
STEW. The audience.
JOE. Burnt to a crisp.
CRITIC. *(Offstage. He moans.)* Uuuuhhhh.
JOE. Except for that one.
STEW. The critic.
JOE. He's in pain, but he's alive. What should we do?
STEW. Let him suffer.
JOE. Something happened, huh?

STEW. Joe, remember the bedtime story Grandpa used to tell us about the humans and the atomic bomb and how we'd be the only ones to survive?
JOE. Uh, no.
STEW. We'd have cookies and milk while he told us?
JOE. Oh, yeah.
STEW. I guess it's true.
JOE. You mean — ?
STEW. Kaboom.
JOE. You mean?
STEW. The end of the human race.
JOE. You mean?
STEW. The end of all the races.
JOE. You mean?
STEW. Except for us.
JOE. You mean?
STEW. The world is ours.
JOE. You mean there won't be an intermission?
STEW. I guess not.
JOE. I wonder what happened to all those snacks.
STEW. How can you think of that right now?
JOE. What — we gotta eat, right?
STEW. Yeah. I guess.
JOE. *(Singing and dancing)*

THIS LAND IS MY LAND.
THIS LAND IS MY LAND.
THIS LAND IS MY LAND.
THIS LAND IS MY LAND.

STEW. What are you so happy about? Except for the suffering and ultimate slow death of the critic, I don't see the cause for joy.
CRITIC. *(Offstage. Moans.)* Ouuuugggg.
JOE. No more humans, right?
STEW. Right.
JOE. That means no more Raid, right?
STEW. Right.
JOE. And no more Combat trays.
STEW. Right.
JOE. No more boric acid mixed with sugar.
STEW. Right.
JOE. No more run for your life here comes a big pair of shoes, right?!!

STEW. Right.

JOE. Well, *shouldn't* we celebrate? I mean we've taken over the world, right?!

STEW. Right.

JOE. Isn't that what we always wanted? Stew, *Stew.* Bye-bye non-profit, hello big bucks! Right? Think of the opportunities. Think of the population explosion. It's unbelievable. We could turn this place into — into the world's first real roach motel. "Where roaches check in, and then they check out."

STEW. Joe.

JOE. Stew.

STEW. You're not thinking of —

JOE. What?

STEW. Not having a theatre?

JOE. Sure I am.

STEW. I'm speechless.

JOE. That's fine.

STEW. Now wait one second, this is a theatre.

JOE. No, this was a theatre.

STEW. Joe.

JOE. Stew.

STEW. I have a something to tell you.

JOE. Yeah?

STEW. I never told this to anyone before.

JOE. Yeah?

STEW. But now seems like a good time. With what's happened.

JOE. Yeah?

STEW. I know we're brothers and all, but I'm well, different.

JOE. You mean — ?

STEW. I'm not like the rest of the family, or even the rest of the species.

JOE. You're not?

STEW. I'm a —

JOE. What?

STEW. A —

JOE. What?

STEW. A —

JOE. *What?*

STEW. A not-for-profit theatre lover.

JOE. What?

STEW. I love this theatre. That's why we've stayed here for so long.

JOE. I thought it was for the brownies and the chocolate chip cookies, and how they didn't have the money to pay someone to clean up the crumbs.
STEW. No. It's the smell of the green room and the roar of the dressing room, the dust on the pile of scripts in the literary office, the broken air conditioning, the young hopeful faces of the interns, the tears of the playwrights —
JOE and STEW. — Especially the ones who get produced.
STEW. The constant begging and demeaning of oneself to raise money, the tyranny of the artistic director — how everyone hates him and kisses his ass at the same time — and of course the rehearsals, the performances, the production meetings, the cast parties.
JOE. At least those are good. Lots of hummus.
STEW. The opening night fundraiser for the board.
JOE. Cheese cubes.
STEW. The only thing I hate, of course, is the critic. *(The Critic, offstage, moans.)*
JOE. I like the critic; he never picks up his candy wrappers.
STEW. I was born in a trunk.
JOE. You were?
STEW. Well, metaphorically. Actually, we were born behind the refrigerator in the artistic director's fabulously tiny deliciously filthy studio apartment. And on the same day that he murdered our mother and father, he unwittingly gave us a new home by carrying us here in his knapsack.
JOE. Things were different then.
STEW. Yes. The plays were daring, the audience was packed, the tickets were cheap, and the critics were so confused by the enthusiasm, they were kind.
JOE. And now we gotta change with the times. Right? No point living in the past. I always wanted to be an entrepreneur. Go into real estate. We could form a partnership. I got lots of ideas. Health clubs, cruise ships, coffee bars. They'll all be dark, damp, and filled with food.
STEW. Joe.
JOE. Stew.
STEW. Haven't you been listening?
JOE. Yeah, haven't you? I mean how many people were in the audience tonight?
STEW. Four. The director, the playwright, the artistic director, the playwright's mother.

JOE. That's not an audience. That's a car pool. *(The Critic, offstage, moans.)*
STEW. And the critic. Five. But I guess he doesn't count. You said humans.
JOE. Look, how big was their debt?
STEW. Big.
JOE. How many fights did they have amongst themselves?
STEW. Many.
JOE. How often were they the butt of jokes in their community?
STEW. Often.
JOE. How badly did the actors try to quit the shows by looking for jobs in the movies?
STEW. Badly.
JOE. Well?
STEW. Well, how bout all the work they've done. That production of *Metamorphosis*? I cried every night.
JOE. I don't remember.
STEW. They served tea with honey in the second act.
JOE. Oh, yeah.
STEW. Think of their dedication to non-commercialism and multiculturalism. The work they did with the disabled, the untalented, the criminally insane. Their commitment in the face of constant failure.
JOE. Stew, this place was a bomb way before the one that dropped in here tonight. I may not be a genius, but I know what I know, and this is not the time and place for a theatre. All you had to do was look at — or crawl over the face of the guy who ran the place. Heartbroken and bitter.
STEW. He dedicated his life to this.
JOE. Exactly. And we survived, and he didn't. Whatever they gave us we lived through it: poison, sterilization, DDT, you name it, we beat it, not by jerking each other off in the name of the theatre. This place? On the evolutionary scale, it thrived for maybe a second. Less.
STEW. But that's why we'd do better.
JOE. Stew, we're talking survival of the fittest, not survival of the artistic! The answer is: No Way. *(Stew starts to sob.)* Oh, geez, don't cry. Look, uh maybe a movie theatre, OK? We could break it into seventy or eighty smaller ones, and call it a a Cockaplex. Or or a porn theatre, all right? With beautiful young roachettes on stage shaking their antennae and showing off their egg sacs. But that's it.
STEW. You don't understand, without this my life has no meaning.
JOE. Oh, come on.

STEW. This is why I survived. I know it.
JOE. Don't be dramatic.
STEW. I'm gonna go electrocute myself on the smoke machine.
JOE. Stew.
STEW. I am. That would be a fitting end; I'll fry myself with the others. If this theatre doesn't survive then I don't. And don't forget who saved who earlier today. *(Stew runs off. He shrieks and moans. Shrieks and moans again.)*
JOE. OK. *(Stew runs back.)*
STEW. Yes?
JOE. OK OK.
STEW. Yes!
JOE. God, all these years I thought you were just a regular roach. Who knew?
STEW. Oh, you won't regret it.
JOE. We'll see about that. So, now what, I mean look at this place, how are we gonna run it?
STEW. Well, well … how many kids do you have?
JOE. I don't know, a few hundred, you?
STEW. The same.
JOE. So?
STEW. Interns!
JOE. Right.
STEW. But my first job as artistic director is to name it. What do you think?
JOE. I don't know. How 'bout Manhattan Roach Club?
STEW. Hmm. Too commercial.
JOE. Lincoln Center Roaches?
STEW. Too overseas.
JOE. Cockroach Horizons?
STEW. Too past its prime.
JOE. Circle Roach Rep?
STEW. Oh no, bad karma there.
JOE. Ensemble Roach Theatre?
STEW. Too neurotic.
JOE. Atlantic Roaches?
STEW. Too robotic.
JOE. Naked Roaches?
STEW. You're kidding, right?
JOE. There'd be good parties. *(Stew shakes his head no.) [Insert name of the theatre where the play is being performed]* — Roaches?

STEW. Hmm. Doesn't ring a bell.
JOE. Well, geez I don't know.
STEW. How 'bout Joe's Theatre?
JOE. Hmm. How 'bout Joe and Stew's Theatre?
STEW. How 'bout Joe and Stew's Theatre of Brotherly Love.
JOE. And Financial Success. Hey, I like that.
STEW. Me too. *(The Critic, offstage, moans.)*
JOE. What's that?
STEW. Oh God.
JOE. Oh no.
STEW. It's the
JOE. Critic!
STEW. He's mutated. He's huge! *(The Critic, offstage, makes indecipherable sounds.)*
JOE. What's he saying?
STEW. He's thanking God for the bomb *(More Critic sounds.)*, that the director and the writer got what they deserved *(Critic sounds.)*, that he's gonna run this place himself and do his favorite shows over and over like *[title of a critically acclaimed play]* and *[another title]. (Critic sounds.)*
JOE and STEW. *(Scream in horror.)* Ahh!
JOE. He's coming our way. We better run.
STEW. I'm not running, this is our home. He can it have over my dead body.
JOE. This is no time for idealism.
STEW. Some things you just gotta stand up for.
JOE. Oh, brother.
STEW. Joe, he's not just a critic.
JOE. He's not?
STEW. No, he represents all the negative forces trying to beat us down, take away our creative spontaneity, and make us feel hopeless and alone. He's the bug in grade school that made fun of the way you scampered, the politician that got elected on hate and fear, the punk that stole your ice cream. Come on, this is the first day of the new world, a chance that'll never come again. Stand still and be counted. He may be big, but we have right against his might. We are brothers for art.
JOE. That's a little cornball, isn't it?
STEW. It was from their last Christmas play, terrible writing, but it seemed apropos, and this guy gave it a good review, worst thing they did all year.

JOE. Here he comes.
STEW. Joe, are you with me?
JOE. Uh.
STEW. We've lived through it all, just like you said —
JOE. Yeah, but.
STEW. It's our theatre, not his!
JOE. It doesn't look that way.
STEW. If we don't take a stand against the critic, who will?
JOE. … We're the only ones left.
STEW. So, are you with me, Joe?
JOE. I'm with you, Stew. *(Stew arms himself with the toothpick.)*
STEW. Well, then. Places! *(They head towards the stage.)*

End of Play

PROPERTY LIST

Broomstick (STEW)

SOUND EFFECTS

Loud explosion

DOTTIE AND RICHIE

DOTTIE AND RICHIE was first performed in the HB Playwrights Theatre's Short Play Festival "The Funeral Plays" 2000 (William Carden, Artistic Director; Pamela Berlin, Playwrights Unit Director) in New York City. It was directed by Suzanne Brinkley; the set design was by Vicki Davis; the costume design was by Amela Baksic and Christopher Peterson; the lighting design was by Renee Molina; the sound design was by Robert Auld; and the production manager was Kim Kefgan. The cast was as follows:

RICHIE .... Mark Nelson
DOTTIE .... Geneva Carr

CHARACTERS

RICHIE, 40. A nice Jewish comedian from Brooklyn. A sweet man with a big heart. He talks quickly, using his hands. Nice on the outside and on the inside. Not to be underestimated.

DOTTIE, 35. Conflicted and confused. With an edge. Trying to do the right thing. For the first time. She thinks she's nice on the outside, but Medusa on the inside.

PLACE

Riverside Memorial Chapel on the Upper West Side of Manhattan.

TIME

December 6, 1999.

DOTTIE AND RICHIE

Richie and Dottie in a room in a funeral parlor. He wears a dark suit. She is in work-out wear.

RICHIE. *(In midstream.)* And it was crowded I mean just people everywhere: Ed Koch, Joan Rivers, Regis, his wife, Joy, Al D'Amato, Claudia Cohen the gossip columnist he went out with, Dr. Judy Kuriansky, a pop psychologist who's been married about twelve times, Joe Franklin. No room downstairs at all, so I got in the elevator and there's Danny Aiello, and Steve Grouper who has this cable access show where people call him up and insult him and that's the whole show, and then I realize I'm standing next to, believe it or not, Imelda Marcos.
DOTTIE. Did you look at her shoes?
RICHIE. No, I didn't even think to, and she was the only one allowed off at the mezzanine, the rest of us weren't, even Jerry Stiller and Anne Meara, who I said hello to 'cause I know them 'cause I met them in East Hampton when I did a comedy festival that they saw and he came up to me afterwards, he thought I was good and asked me to write something for his roast — did you see it? — so I did. Anyway he used a sentence of mine, which was nice, and Anne Meara who I had previously met years ago when she said a very strange thing to me, anyway the rest of us, including Joy Behar, got off at the third floor after Imelda was gone, and I'm usually not too pushy but I managed to get my way onto the balcony and stood right next to Caroline Hirsch who owns Carolines, Abe Beame, and Peter Max, I think it was Peter Max, and I had a perfect view.
DOTTIE. Good.
RICHIE. And people spoke, and kept referring to the mayor and the first lady, and I thought it was Hillary, but I guess it was just Donna, and the mayor got up and made this awful joke about how he tried to take a cab over, but no one would stop and pick him up. And uh Cindy, Joey's wife, said something about Sirio letting them have a good table at Le Cirque even during Joey's last days when he

wasn't eating well. I guess that's her idea of a great act of humanitarianism. And the rabbi, of course, and then some kind of a minister who said "the last time I saw Joey, he was in a wheelchair and when I asked him if he was comfortable he said … I make a living." Which was funny, old but funny, and then he said it a second time, which wasn't so funny.

DOTTIE. Uh huh.

RICHIE. I just felt it was important for me to be here. To pay my respects. I mean Joey was a friar, I'm a friar, he was a comic, I'm a comic. And he had me on his radio show once. In the eighties.

DOTTIE. Uh huh.

RICHIE. I haven't been to a funeral since Mr. Henny Youngman passed. And it struck me, how death is the big equalizer, you know? I mean, Imelda Marcos, Michael Musto, Mathilda Cuomo, and me, all here on December 6th, 1999. To mark the death of Joey Adams.

DOTTIE. Yeah?

RICHIE. And then I thought of you. And last night. I couldn't stop thinking about you. Seeing you. How amazing it was. And I remembered I left my wallet. At your place. So right after the service ended, I called. And here you are. Thanks for coming by.

DOTTIE. Sure.

RICHIE. I would have been happy to come over.

DOTTIE. This place is a block from my gym. And I was about to go work out.

RICHIE. You look beautiful.

DOTTIE. I didn't even shower.

RICHIE. You not showering is beautiful.

DOTTIE. You're sweet.

RICHIE. No, you are.

DOTTIE. You're very sweet.

RICHIE. I had a great time.

DOTTIE. Yeah?

RICHIE. I've never — I mean — I don't know how to say this — I've never had a night like that, I never felt that, and I've been with other women and. I have no words. For me, that's something. I even lost my appetite. I was hungry and we still, and then we ate — after. I'm just so happy to see you.

DOTTIE. Yeah?

RICHIE. Maybe we could go for a bite to eat? Now that I have my wallet back. Maybe a tuna sandwich, a nice pasta, or a salad, something light. I know you like to eat light, I'd like to like to eat light. I

mean I know I had a steak last night, with french fries and blue cheese dressing. And cake. But I could eat light. Like Thai or Italian or.
DOTTIE. Look.
RICHIE. I am. I could look at you a lot. I could look at you today, I could look at you tomorrow. Oh, tomorrow. I'm doing a benefit, with Professor Irwin Corey at the Jewish Home for the Aged on the West Side, maybe I could come over after. I know it's more than a block away, but it is on the west side, and you're on the west side. And next week I'm hosting a singles variety show at the Y. I could interview you.
DOTTIE. I wouldn't know what to say.
RICHIE. I'm sure they'd love to just look at you. Dottie.
DOTTIE. Richie?
RICHIE. Dottie.
DOTTIE. Richie.
RICHIE. I just want to touch you and smother you with kisses and be with you and spend all day together and all night and all day and —
DOTTIE. I'm not really that great.
RICHIE. Oh, you are.
DOTTIE. No, I I have bad feet. They get tired, and I have to sit down a lot.
RICHIE. I love to sit.
DOTTIE. And my apartment —
RICHIE. — A palace.
DOTTIE. I don't shave my legs.
RICHIE. I couldn't tell.
DOTTIE. Or under my arms.
RICHIE. I noticed a lovely fuzz.
DOTTIE. And the way I have to, you know, in order to —
RICHIE. — It's my pleasure to serve.
DOTTIE. I'm still stuck on my ex.
RICHIE. I can handle that.
DOTTIE. He was a cross-dresser.
RICHIE. I can see why it ended.
DOTTIE. I have overwhelming feelings of rage towards any man I'm with.
RICHIE. Who said life was easy?
DOTTIE. Bad relationship history, you know, psychotics, addicts, pathological liars. The terminally ill.
RICHIE. Then perhaps you're ready for a change.

DOTTIE. I've been considering becoming a lesbian.
RICHIE. I'd love to hear all about it.
DOTTIE. Allergic to pets.
RICHIE. Maybe a nice poodle, hair not fur, you know?
DOTTIE. A polyp in my uterus.
RICHIE. I'll be there for the surgery. Dottie, you bring out the best in me.
DOTTIE. Richie, how is it you're still single?
RICHIE. 'Cause I never met a girl like you. You're who I always dreamed of, but never knew. 'Til last night. *(He touches her.)* I wish this were a nice bed and breakfast and we could go upstairs, order in, and then I'd kiss you *(He kisses her.)* and touch you. *(He touches her.)* And take off your clothes. *(He's all over her.)*
DOTTIE. *(She pulls away.)* I killed Joey Adams.
RICHIE. Excuse me?
DOTTIE. I killed him.
RICHIE. What do you mean?
DOTTIE. It was me.
RICHIE. You are speaking, I take it, in a metaphorical type of way.
DOTTIE. I am not who you think I am. As wonderful as last night was, that's how awful it will get.
RICHIE. And uh the fact that he was eighty-eight years old and had cancer, this had nothing to do with how he died?
DOTTIE. There are lots of ways it can happen.
RICHIE. What exactly is going on here?
DOTTIE. I am not your dream girl. In fact I'm your worst nightmare. I don't even look like this. This is just me in the beginning. When the trap is being set. Then, maybe it'll be an accident. A burn from coffee that's too hot, a depression that leads to suicide. Stand-up comic slips on a banana peel and falls through a chasm to his demise. Funnyboy, don't let me touch your funny bone again. 'Cause you'll be crying your way back here from the inside of your very own box. You get where I'm coming from? You keep away or you'll go the way of Joey Deadman Not Walking Adams. He's greeting the grubs and meeting the maggots. I saw his last act, and he didn't kill. I did. So be a stand-up guy, and open your eyes, 'cause I'm coming your way. Plane crash? It's probably me. Arson? I've arrived. Succubus? I'm by your side. So, nice man, Mr. Comedian, who likes to make 'em laugh, you with the stars in your eyes and the swell in your pants, run away I say, before it's too late. And I throw my long locks over the side of the castle, then take off

my wig and watch you tumble down to hell.
RICHIE. I appreciate you have some uh intimacy issues.
DOTTIE. Intimacy?
RICHIE. I was thinking if maybe we could just let things develop, you know in a natural way.
DOTTIE. Natural, what's natural? Look around, what do you see? The leftovers, the skins, the once-wet-now-dried formaldehydes of those that dared to love me.
RICHIE. You wanna get something to eat and talk about this?
DOTTIE. I will devour you for breakfast and spit you out at lunch.
RICHIE. You did say you were in therapy, right? Is it once a week or twice?
DOTTIE. Fool. I am warning you to get your clown feet in highest gear and get the hell out of here. *(A beat. He steps away. Then back.)*
RICHIE. Why are you telling me this?
DOTTIE. Don't look a gift horse in the mouth.
RICHIE. If it were true, why would you say?
DOTTIE. No reason.
RICHIE. Nonsense … I'm not going anywhere until you answer.
DOTTIE. A warning, OK?
RICHIE. But why?
DOTTIE. 'Cause you're sweet.
RICHIE. What do you know from sweet except it tastes good? You liked me.
DOTTIE. I like no man.
RICHIE. It was different this time.
DOTTIE. It's always different: car crash, cancer, broken bungee cord. I don't get bored.
RICHIE. Admit it. You liked me.
DOTTIE. I felt pity.
RICHIE. A monster like you?
DOTTIE. Skip the flattery.
RICHIE. You like me.
DOTTIE. An absurdity.
RICHIE. I win.
DOTTIE. Excuse me?
RICHIE. You may have killed Joey Adams, but I *am Joey Adams*. And all those that came before him. And I'm still here. It didn't work, see? I'm still listening. I'm still breathing. I'm still making jokes. I'm not riddled with bullets. I am the riddle. I keep coming back. Ice me, and I melt. Kill me, and I laugh. Your fatal bite gives

me delight. Your venom tastes like nectar. You're not so bad.

DOTTIE. I lure them in like honey, then watch them drop like flies.

RICHIE. Well, I'm not much of an insect myself.

DOTTIE. You will regret this day.

RICHIE. I know what I felt.

DOTTIE. You felt what I wanted you to feel.

RICHIE. I saw it in your face.

DOTTIE. You saw what you wanted to see.

RICHIE. You think I'm stupid? You think I'm weak? You think I don't know what I'm doing? I beat you at your own game. You softened. Under my breath. I was there.

DOTTIE. Nonsense.

RICHIE. You warned me. You warned me. You care. I could see it in your eyes, I could taste it on your lips. It's been an eternity. But I win. You're mine. I'm yours. The end.

DOTTIE. It was just a ploy.

RICHIE. You took off your own peel, and you slipped, sweetie. You made a mistake.

DOTTIE. You didn't realize.

RICHIE. *You* didn't realize.

DOTTIE. You made a mistake.

RICHIE. It's over.

DOTTIE. No, it's not.

RICHIE. You're right. It's just beginning.

DOTTIE. No, it's not. It's over.

RICHIE. Then why don't you just walk away?

DOTTIE. You.

RICHIE. You.

DOTTIE. You.

RICHIE. You.

DOTTIE. *You.*

RICHIE. *You.*

DOTTIE. You.

RICHIE. You.

DOTTIE. You.

RICHIE. You. *(They lean in to kiss. They both pull away. They lean in to kiss. They stop, lips almost touching. Blackout.)*

End of Play

FOR-EVERETT

FOR-EVERETT was first performed in the HB Playwrights Theatre's Short Play Festival 2002 (William Carden, Artistic Director; Pamela Berlin, Playwrights Unit Director) in New York City. It was directed by Mark Nelson; the set design was by Michael Schweikardt; the costume design was by Linda Ross; the lighting design was by Chris Dallos; the sound design was by Sten Severson; and the production manager was David Apichell. The cast was as follows:

CATHERINE .... Betsy Aidem
EVERETT .... Conan McCarty
KIRK .... Matte Osian

CHARACTERS

CATHERINE, 40ish.

EVERETT, 40ish. Catherine's ex. Nine years together, three apart.

KIRK, 40ish. Had a fling with Catherine twelve years ago. Then calls her up. He likes her.

TIME

Jumps around.

PLACE

Jumps around.

NOTE: It's best to do this play with no props.

FOR-EVERETT

A beach. Catherine and Everett onstage. They look at each other. Everett walks upstage towards the ocean, turns and looks back at her three times, each time with the sound of a camera shutter click.

EVERETT. I'm going in. You coming with me?
CATHERINE. Uh.
EVERETT. I'm going in. Come with me! *(She talks to the audience:)*
CATHERINE. I have these three photographs. I took them. Years ago. Everett was walking away, looking back at me, going towards the water.
EVERETT. You coming?
CATHERINE. Big smile. Sad around the eyes. Slight stomach, showing he's not perfect, even now, to me, he doesn't look … perfect. *(She looks at him.)* Beautiful man … You know those pictures that you have, that you can't look at, 'cause they break your heart? Well, anything with him in it, does that. I took those maybe ten years ago. Yet, I look at the ocean today, what do I see — Everett.
EVERETT. Are you coming in?
CATHERINE. You know how you go to the beach, especially when you're a kid and at home the sand is everywhere you can't get rid of it? In your shoes your sheets your teeth? That uninvited crunch when you eat those cherries? Look at him. *(To Everett:)* Hey.
EVERETT. Hey.
CATHERINE. Maybe if we could do it again.
EVERETT. What?
CATHERINE. That moment, could we do it again?
EVERETT. I don't see how.
CATHERINE. Maybe *I* could just do it again.
EVERETT. By yourself?
CATHERINE. See, if we could, if I could, I'd open my arms, nod my head and smile every day. I'd say I was happy just having

you near me … But of course I can't. You can't. So. Really — *(Lights brighten as Everett exits and Kirk appears upstage.)* — It's years later, and I'm here, with another man, the kind of man that I should know better, at this age, hell, shouldn't I know better, but it's like it always is, or only is once in a while now, like the undertow like you can't help it, it's his smell or his height or the way he has to bend down 'cause he's tall or how he's late all the time and you hate that or how he's smarter than you thought or how his face looks like a boy's in spite of itself, and how he just appeared, really, out of nowhere, from the past, the long ago past, you met him first, before you even met Everett, and all the signals say no and yet you want to go, you feel pulled, even though you think no, don't, no: high tide, and I don't swim well, not in those kind of waves, not anymore, no.

KIRK. Hey, I'm going in. You want to come?

CATHERINE. *(Frozen.)* Oh. Uh.

KIRK. Come with me. I'm going in.

CATHERINE. Um.

KIRK. Hey, sweetheart, are you coming?

CATHERINE. Uh. *(Lights change and music, maybe Tom Petty's "Free Falling," plays.* * *To audience:)* Twelve years ago, I came here, to this island, for a weeklong vacation. I was sitting in a bar, and this stunning gazelle of a guy walked in. I'd been watching Becker and Lendl, but deserted them for him — coming my way. I felt this blonde heat, I smelled the salt on his skin, he'd probably just come from this very beach.

KIRK. *(To bartender:)* Hey Joe, can I get a beer and a burger?

CATHERINE. Of course he eats meat.

KIRK. Yeah, rare.

CATHERINE. Of course he wants it rare. Probably lives around here. The kind of tall, handsome guy that would never talk to me.

KIRK. *(To her:)* Hi.

CATHERINE. *(To him:)* Hi. *(To audience:)* Did he just say hi?

KIRK. Hi. I'm Kirk.

CATHERINE. Hi. Kirk. *(Out:)* He's not wearing underwear. I don't know that 'til later. After he's bought me a couple of Mudslides then taught me the best way to have fun at the Sunlight Inn after dark.

KIRK. Hi.

* See Special Note on Songs and Recordings on copyright page.

CATHERINE. When he takes off his clothes, he looks — perfect. He is my very own Ken doll, while I'm one of Barbie's wannabe friends, without the feet molded for high heels.
KIRK. Hi.
CATHERINE. He comes to my room every night for a week; I sleep during the day. I feel like a sex bat.
KIRK. Mmm.
CATHERINE. I keep hoping he'll invite me to come back and visit. I drop so many hints I feel like I've lost weight. But he doesn't. *(Kirk walks away.)* Invite me. And the week's over. I go home. I don't hear from him. *(She looks at Kirk. He exits.)* And soon after, I meet someone else. I meet Everett. *(Everett appears. Music. They embrace.)* I don't know how to stop missing Everett. *(They gently dance.)* He and I did this push-me-pull-you dance for almost a decade. 'Til someone pushed or pulled too hard too many times, and he went out — *(They stop dancing. Music out. Everett drifts off.)* — to sea. I hear he lost his way; caught in a storm, trapped by a rough current, still looking for the shore. I don't know how to stop missing Everett. Feels like for-everett. I've spent the last year trying not to call him. Well, really, it's been two years. OK, actually, three. For 1,038 days, it's become part of my daily life, an occupation: eating, sleeping, and not calling Everett. *(The phone rings.)* Whenever the phone rings, I wonder is it —
KIRK. *(Appears.)* Hi, it's Kirk, remember me?
CATHERINE. Kirk?
KIRK. Hi. It's been a long time. I'm in town. I'd like to see you.
CATHERINE. As in Kirk, the guy I met twelve years ago and never heard from? No way.
KIRK. Hi. Kirk again.
CATHERINE. One syllable. Kirk.
KIRK. Oh, elusive one — where are you?
CATHERINE. Direct. Persistent.
KIRK. Hi.
CATHERINE. A friend of mine said if the relationship is all in your head, if the other person isn't actually with you, if you have to act out both parts, then it isn't a relationship. I pick up the phone. *(Too loud.)* Just so you know, I'm not the young hottie I was back then. I'll be the middle-aged woman waiting out front.
KIRK. You look great. Dinner was great. I'll walk you home.
CATHERINE. You're not coming upstairs with me. Just so it's clear, OK?

KIRK. Yeah, OK.
CATHERINE. Good night.
KIRK. Can I kiss you? *(He does. She jumps on him.)* Whoa.
CATHERINE. *(Out:)* I remember why I liked him.
KIRK. When I like someone, I think about how I can please them. I think I once pleased you.
CATHERINE. *(Out:)* He's making it up, right?
KIRK. I want to cook for you. Steak.
CATHERINE. I don't really eat steak.
KIRK. Chicken? Fish?
CATHERINE. Well, OK. *(Kirk cries.)* What is it?
KIRK. Oh, I was just thinking about my father. He died recently and —
CATHERINE. *(Out:)* I'm so moved by his tears but also think he's trying to gain my trust so he can take all my money then kill me in various ways that have to do with kissing or touching or having someone cook for you. I wipe his eyes. *(Lights out.)*
KIRK and CATHERINE. Sex talk, sex talk, sex talk. Sex talk, sex talk, sex talk. *(Lights up. They look ridiculously disheveled.)*
KIRK. I'm rusty.
CATHERINE. You are?
KIRK. I've been alone for quite a while.
CATHERINE. You have? *(Out:)* I'm thinking: ex-con, pedophile, gambler, liar, slacker, spy. *(To him:)* Why?
KIRK. Hey, I'm gonna fix your place up. I'll fix your switches. I'll install new outlets. Change your lock. How 'bout a massage. You got oil?
CATHERINE. He's kidding, right? *(Lights out.)*
CATHERINE and KIRK. Sex talk sex talk sex talk. Sex talk sex talk sex talk! *(Lights up.)*
KIRK. Hey, I'm putting in that new lock.
CATHERINE. Ah! My door. It's in pieces.
KIRK. Don't worry —
CATHERINE. — But —
KIRK. Just a little problem. Getting it to fit. Trust me. I'll put it back together. There.
CATHERINE. *(Out:)* My door. My totally banged-up door. *(To him:)* Thanks.
KIRK. I'll meet you at eight.
CATHERINE. Where were you?
KIRK. I'll call you at six.

CATHERINE. You didn't.
KIRK. I'll be there at seven.
CATHERINE. You weren't.
KIRK. This time I'll be on time —
CATHERINE. I waited. You can't keep saying you're gonna do something, then not do it.
KIRK. Won't happen again. I'll be there at eight.
CATHERINE. *You didn't show up? Where were you? You cannot just not show up, then come over and show up! You're not staying. It's late.*
KIRK. I went back 'cause I forgot these. For you. Here. White cherries. They looked perfect. I thought of you.
CATHERINE. Oh.
KIRK. Try one.
CATHERINE. *(She eats one.)* Oh oh.
KIRK. And I got you this. *(Music. Maybe the chorus of The Stylistics' "You Are Everything" plays.*)* I want to slow-dance with you. Come on. Come here. I'm sorry. *(They dance.)* I could fall in love with you. *(Lights out.)*
CATHERINE. *(Yells.)* Did you give me a disease!? You gave me a disease do you have any diseases I know you gave me a disease and if you're lying I'll find out 'cause I'm going to the doctor and she'll tell me so you better tell the truth 'cause if you don't I'll really be mad.
KIRK. I don't have any diseases. Not that I know of. *(Lights up.)*
CATHERINE. Not that you know of, what good is that, not that you know of, what do you know of, I mean what do you know, you don't know, what do you know! *(Out.)* I think he's going to kill me, I really do. He's tall and he could kill me. He wears a Leatherman. On his belt.
KIRK. Here, I got you this. Here. And this. Here. I got you this. Here. For you. This. This. For you.
CATHERINE. I talked to the doctor. I'm fine. I'm sorry.
KIRK. All of this. For you.
CATHERINE. There's something that is just so … manly. I look at you and you are just so manly.
KIRK. While I'm sautéing mushrooms?
CATHERINE. Yes.
KIRK. Control. I'm in control.
CATHERINE. Of the mushrooms?

* See Special Note on Songs and Recordings on copyright page.

KIRK. Yeah.
CATHERINE. *(Realization.)* Oh. You are. Oh.
KIRK. I'm leaving on Monday.
CATHERINE. Shrimp and mushrooms.
KIRK. I'm not gonna go 'til Friday.
CATHERINE. Salmon and mushrooms.
KIRK. I'm staying 'til —
CATHERINE. Swordfish, cod, and scrod with mushrooms.
KIRK. — Tuesday.
CATHERINE. I'm well fed.
KIRK. — Definitely going by —
CATHERINE. — overfed.
KIRK. — Saturday.
CATHERINE. Stuffed really.
KIRK. Or Sunday.
CATHERINE. I have to ask him to go. Sorry. I'm sorry. But go. You have to go. *(He exits.)* He's gone. Finally. He's gone. God, I miss him. *(We hear music, maybe "You are Everything" again. Sound of a phone dialing.)* Hi, I wanted to say hi. To talk. You left and. I was just thinking about you and. Give me a call. We left things kind of um open-ended and. Call me. Everett. Please call. *(Out:)* You'd think after three years I'd have noticed that the open end had closed, or at the very least narrowed. *(The phone rings.)* Hello? *(Lights change. A repeat of the earlier moment at the beach. The same lights, same staging.)*
KIRK. *(From upstage.)* Hey, I'm going in. You want to come?
CATHERINE. *(Frozen.)* Oh. Uh.
KIRK. Come with me. I'm going in.
CATHERINE. Um.
KIRK. Hey, sweetheart, are you coming?
CATHERINE. Uh. *(To audience:)* So. I'm here with Kirk. He called. To invite me. Back to this beach. After twelve years. By that calculation, maybe I'll hear from Everett in another — nine. *(Everett appears. To Everett:)* Hey.
EVERETT. Hey.
CATHERINE. I still see you. *(He nods.)* I'm still seeing you. Some things just don't get better.
KIRK. Are you coming in?
EVERETT. Are you?
CATHERINE. With him? I don't know. I keep thinking he wants to kill me. I mean he hasn't. Yet. But. Out there? I don't even like

to get my face wet. *(Out:)* You know that first time when you're body surfing, catching the waves and suddenly you're caught, you're tossed, can't see can't breathe, can't find up or down; it feels like forever or it's only a second? *(To Everett:)* Hey.

EVERETT. Hey.

KIRK. Hey.

CATHERINE. *(To Everett:)* I'd go with you. Right now. I'd open my arms, nod my head, and smile every day.

EVERETT. You wouldn't say that if you'd been with me the last three years.

CATHERINE. I would.

EVERETT. You made the right choice. Back then.

CATHERINE. Why didn't you call?

EVERETT. 'Cause I don't want to talk to you.

CATHERINE. Then why don't you go away?

EVERETT. Sweetie, I'm not even here.

CATHERINE. Where are you?

EVERETT. Not with you. He is.

KIRK. Are you coming?

EVERETT. Catherine.

CATHERINE. Everett.

KIRK. Catherine.

EVERETT. Some things —

CATHERINE. — Don't get better.

EVERETT. I'm not even here.

KIRK. The water's great!

EVERETT. Why not?

CATHERINE. But.

KIRK. Let's go!

EVERETT. Go ahead.

KIRK. Come on!

EVERETT. Come on.

CATHERINE. But.

KIRK. I'm goin'!

EVERETT. Just get your feet wet.

CATHERINE. But.

EVERETT. Go.

KIRK. Go.

CATHERINE. But.

EVERETT. Go. *(Catherine steps upstage, towards the ocean. She turns and looks back at Everett. Sound of a camera shutter click. She steps towards the water, then looks back at Everett again. Click. The third time, she looks at the audience, with a shrug and a slight smile. Click. Blackout.)*

End of Play

SOUND EFFECTS

Sound of camera shutter clicking
Music
Phone ringing
Phone being dialed

2B (OR NOT 2B)

2B (OR NOT 2B) was first fully staged at the Actors Theatre of Louisville in Kentucky on February 2, 2005. It was directed by Erica Bradshaw; the set design was by Brenda Ellis; the costume design was by Kevin Thacker; the lighting design was by Matt Cross and Katie McCreary; the props were by Joe Cunningham and Deanna Hilleman; and the dramaturg was JoSelle Vanderhooft. The cast was as follows:

FRANNY .... Anna Bollard
DAVE THE BEE .... Ian Frank

2B (OR NOT 2B) had a staged reading in "Acts of Love," a benefit for Cure Autism Now, at the Canon Theatre in Beverly Hills, California, on October 20, 2003. It was directed by David Tochterman. The cast was as follows:

FRANNY .... Julie Warner
DAVE THE BEE .... Patrick Warburton

CHARACTERS

FRANNY, a woman in her 30s

A BEE, a male bee named Dave

PLACE

Franny's studio apartment in Upper Manhattan.

TIME

Now.

2B (OR NOT 2B)

Franny, upset, disheveled, in her studio apartment, on the phone and waxing her legs.

FRANNY. I know you told me it was over and I respect that I mean I understand it and I know you don't want to see me again and I know I was not very nice to you — at times — and I just want to say that I've had a well a complete not-nice-ostomy and a total unlike-ectomy, I've had all the not nice unlikable parts removed so if you call me I'm sure we can work it out. *(She hangs up. She tears off a strip of wax from her legs.)* AH! *(She cries. She dials. She holds the receiver to her leg. She rips wax.)* Ah! I'm waxing my legs. I know you hated my hairy legs, so I'm waxing! I can't believe you haven't called me back. *(Hangs up. Rips off more wax.)* Ah! *(Dials.)* I heard you asked out my friend Eleanor, and I thought you'd like to know she has the papilloma virus — in her vagina. And in her mouth. On her tongue. In case you happened to have kissed her already. Wouldn't worry about it though, I'm sure it's fine … OK, well, thanks for breaking my heart. And I still really love you and if you want to change your mind and give it another try, let me know. *(Hangs up. Cries. Rips wax.)* Ah! *(A human-sized bee appears.)* AHH!! *(She hides her head, she looks.)* Ohmigod-ohmigodohmigod! *(She tries to hide. The bee is huge. There's nowhere to go. She runs into a corner.)* Ohmigod. OK. Could you just go? Please. Um. Shoo. Go. *(He doesn't budge.)* Look, the park is a few blocks away, if you could just fly over there. I'm sure you'd be happier. *(He doesn't move. She crouches to the floor. Or hides under the bed.)* Or or in the back, there's a garden. With uh plants. Or, my neighbor, downstairs, she has these window boxes: geraniums, impatiens. I'm sure you're in the wrong place.
BEE. Is this 2B?
FRANNY. What?
BEE. 2B or not 2B?
FRANNY. It's a joke, right?

BEE. I wouldn't make a joke like that.
FRANNY. OK, this is 2B, but I'm sure it's the wrong building.
BEE. 344 West 188 Street?
FRANNY. *(Grabs her bag, and tosses it at the bee.)* OK, take whatever you want. I only have ten dollars, but I'll write down my PIN number. My bank's on the corner, you can have it all.
BEE. I don't want your money.
FRANNY. Then take the Tivo. Or or the organic honey, OK?
BEE. I don't want that.
FRANNY. Look, I'm possibly allergic. And my epipen will not be of much use in this case cause you are ohmigod so fucking big you are the biggest bee I have ever seen. I can't believe this is happening. *(She grabs the phone.)* Frank. Help! There's a giant bee in my apartment. Could you come over? Please!
BEE. He's a jerk. Forget about him.
FRANNY. What?
BEE. You deserve better.
FRANNY. Well, thank you, I will consider that. Now please, go away. Or I'll call the police.
BEE. I don't think they'll come for a bee.
FRANNY. I am really afraid of you. I mean really afraid. Bees are my well thing you know some people it's snakes or heights or whatever, but me, it's bees.
BEE. I won't hurt you.
FRANNY. Well that's nice to hear but.
BEE. Why would I hurt you?
FRANNY. I don't know. Because you're a bee.
BEE. Have you been hurt before?
FRANNY. Yes.
BEE. Yellow jackets.
FRANNY. No, bee. Bees. I've been stung. So I am sure you are in the wrong apartment.
BEE. It's the right apartment.
FRANNY. Then it's the wrong species. I'm a human, a female human, and and you're not invited.
BEE. How's that going for you?
FRANNY. What?
BEE. Being a female human?
FRANNY. It's fine. It's just fine.
BEE. Work and love, it's all good? How's your job? *(Franny sneaks towards the window while talking.)*

FRANNY. Fine. I'm a receptionist. It's a career change. I used to be a painter. Very cutting edge, I didn't even use paint, I used body fluids, but um it didn't work out because several others already claimed that niche, you wouldn't believe what some people do with their menstrual blood, so now I uh have a job and a boss and uh — *(She can't get out the window.)*
BEE. And your human female love life? *(Franny crawls all around the room, heading towards a certain cabinet while talking.)*
FRANNY. Well my first relationships were with typical self-involved commitmentphobes when I was between the ages of say, five and twelve. Then junior high was alcoholics, high school was drug addicts, college: gay men, a guy who owned a duck, then a physically challenged interpretive ice skater, meaning, you know, an amputee who'd skate with a kind of stick with a blade at the bottom, then I married a guy who liked to put garlic in his ears, but I went away a lot with my boyfriend who was a puppeteer for the blind, then my husband fell for a woman with short limbs, and I got pregnant but lost the baby, and the father, well, he was a midwesterner, so, then I had a slew of internet dates with incredibly boring men which is I guess a sign of getting older — the men tell long stories that sound like intricate recipes on how to marinate poultry. *(Franny has now snuck around to her cabinet, pulled out a can of bug spray, and points it at the bee.)* OK. Get out. Or I will spray you with this deadly spray. *(She sprays. The can is empty. She shakes, tries again, nothing.)* Damn. *(She runs for the door. It won't open.)*
BEE. You like flowers, don't you, Franny?
FRANNY. How do you know my name?
BEE. *(Pulls out a bouquet.)* And tulips are your favorite, aren't they?
FRANNY. How do you — ? OK. Thanks for the delivery. You can put those down — over there. And now you can go.
BEE. Do you know how intoxicatingly beautiful you are?
FRANNY. Now, that's a joke.
BEE. We find you unbearably sexy.
FRANNY. Who's we?
BEE. We know you haven't even begun to tap into your erotic capacity.
FRANNY. What's that smell?
BEE. That's my nectar.
FRANNY. Mmm. Not bad.

BEE. Franny Dambrose, you are wonderfully demanding, fascinatingly moody, exquisitely impossible to please.
FRANNY. Well —
BEE. Complicated, codependent and controlling. Perfect in all ways.
FRANNY. Well —
BEE. We want to give you everything you always wanted, but thought you couldn't have: love, fulfillment, hot sex; we will serve your every need.
FRANNY. Well.
BEE. We want you to be our Queen.
FRANNY. What?
BEE. We've watched you. We've chosen you. We know you.
FRANNY. What is this?
BEE. You can run, but you can't hive. We even have a sense of humor.
FRANNY. Hardly.
BEE. Just think: You wouldn't have to work. You'd have plenty of time: to read, to lounge, to do your art. Think what you could paint with pollen.
FRANNY. That's very nice of you, but, hey why don't you get um, a real bee? I know you could find one, in um the park.
BEE. We had a bad experience. She was a … killer. So we've opted for this scientifically advanced entomologically evolutionary revolutionary solution. We find a very special human female and offer her a better life. Works well for all involved.
FRANNY. If it works so well, what happened to your last one?
BEE. She fell in love with a wasp. Not recommended. The children will be confused.
FRANNY. OK.
BEE. Franny, imagine yourself. As Queen. You'd never be alone again on a Friday night. You'd be serving the greater good by helping to cross-pollinate. Not to mention, we will please you in every way. Have you ever thought about being with more than one male and their only pleasure is your pleasure?
FRANNY. Well. Um. Look, it's nothing personal, but I find you, I'm sorry to say, physically, uh, repulsive.
BEE. Oh, I think that could change.
FRANNY. And, I'm human.
BEE. That, too, can change. Amelia Earhart? She didn't disappear. She made a choice. So can you.

FRANNY. But what's wrong with being human?
BEE. Have you read the paper lately? Your species isn't exactly living up to its potential.
FRANNY. Amelia Earhart?
BEE. I don't want to rush you Franny, except that my brothers and cousins are eagerly waiting and time is quickly running out. Don't you want what I've offered? What is it you're reluctant to give up?
FRANNY. Well. My apartment.
BEE. A studio in Inwood?
FRANNY. It's near the subway.
BEE. You'd have your own hive.
FRANNY. My job.
BEE. That job sucks.
FRANNY. There are perks.
BEE. Like what?
FRANNY. Uh … frequent flyer miles.
BEE. You won't need those.
FRANNY. And there's Frank.
BEE. Frank is a fly, a gnat, a roach. Besides he's an actor. Forget Frank.
FRANNY. Believe me I've tried.
BEE. Franny oh Franny, have you looked at your life lately?
FRANNY. I prefer not to.
BEE. All of your qualities that absolutely don't work as a female human will work like gangbusters as a bee.
FRANNY. Things'll get better.
BEE. How long have you been saying that?
FRANNY. Time heals all wounds.
BEE. Then why are you still hurting? And why are you inflicting excruciating pain to your lovely legs? We like fuzzy!
FRANNY. Really?
BEE. Really. Weren't you the Queen in your grade-school play? Didn't you enjoy it?
FRANNY. I loved it. But I didn't get to keep the crown. I wanted that crown.
BEE. You could have a crown.
FRANNY. But. Still. I'm terrified of you. I see a bee, I flee. It's a kind of a flight or flight kind of thing. I don't go on picnics, I avoid practically the entire outdoors because of you.
BEE. What exactly are you afraid of?
FRANNY. Pain, death, dying alone, that sort of thing.

BEE. Touch my stinger.
FRANNY. What?
BEE. Touch it.
FRANNY. No.
BEE. Don't you think it's time to change?
FRANNY. That's a pretty big change.
BEE. I know you, Franny Dambrose. The reason you're afraid of me is because you are me. In your heart, you're a bee. Touch it. *(She touches it. Pulls her hand away. Twice. Touches it.)*
FRANNY. Oh. Oh. It's — it's nice.
BEE. Isn't it?
FRANNY. It's mmm warm.
BEE. Yes.
FRANNY. Powerful.
BEE. Yes.
FRANNY. It's … growing.
BEE. Yes.
FRANNY. And that smell. Your... nectar.
BEE. Yes. *(A musical humming is heard. Lights change.)*
FRANNY. That sound. What is it?
BEE. My cousins and brothers. Here to serve you.
FRANNY. Oh my. *(She feels them all over her body.)* What are they doing?
BEE. Touching you, tickling you, trying to please you.
FRANNY. Oh. Oh. *(The bee puts yellow stripes on her.)* What're those?
BEE. Your stripes.
FRANNY. They're so … soft. *(He puts antennae on her.)* Oh. *(He puts wings on her.)* Oh. They're beautiful. I. Oh. *(The bee kisses her.)*
FRANNY. I can't believe I kissed a bee. I feel … different. What's your name?
BEE. Dave the Bee.
FRANNY. Hi, Dave. *(The phone rings.)*
BEE. Let it ring.
FRANNY. But. *(Ring.)*
BEE. Forget it.
FRANNY. But. *(Ring.)* It might be my boss. Or.
BEE. It's time.
FRANNY. But.
BEE. Let's go.
FRANNY. What if it's Frank?! *(She answers the phone.)* Hello?

Frank? *(The lights change. The humming stops.)* I'm glad you called. What? You want me to stop calling? You're really happy since we broke up? You're still seeing my friend Eleanor? You've asked her to marry you!? Great. That's just great. (*As Franny is about to burst into tears and launch an attack, Dave puts a crown on her head. And voila. She is transformed. She nearly drops the phone.)* Frank, remember the Don't-bee and the Do-bee? Well, you are most definitely a Don't. And when it comes to you and your kind, I am done. *(She hangs up. She dials again.)* Buzz off!! *(She hangs up. Humming sounds. Lights change. Music. She kisses Dave.)* OK, boys, let's fly.

End of Play

PROPERTY LIST

Phone (FRANNY)
Waxing strips (FRANNY)
Bag (FRANNY)
Spray can (FRANNY)
Bouquet of tulips (BEE)
Yellow stripes (BEE)
Antennae (BEE)
Wings (BEE)
Crown (BEE)

SOUND EFFECTS

Phone ring
Musical humming

JILEY NANCE AND LEDNERG

JILEY NANCE AND LEDNERG was first performed in the HB Playwrights Theatre's Short Play Festival 2001, "The Hospital Plays," (William Carden, Artistic Director; Pamela Berlin, Playwrights Unit Director) in New York City. It was directed by Ethan Silverman; the set design was by Michael Schweikardt; the costume design was by Mary Margaret O'Neill; the lighting design was by John Lassiter; the sound design was by John Kadela; and the production manager was David Apichell. The cast was as follows:

JILEY NANCE .... Nancy Giles
LEDNERG .... Cecilia deWolf

CHARACTERS

JILEY NANCE, 40. Tall, smart, funny, lovely woman.

LEDNERG, old nasty creature. She is a monster in disguise, pretending to be nice.

PLACE

Hospital room.

TIME

Now.

JILEY NANCE AND LEDNERG

Lights up on a hospital room with two beds and a curtain drawn between them. Grendel is in the far bed, sucking on some bones. She tosses a bone into a bucket. Jiley enters with an overnight bag. Grendel watches Jiley through the curtain as Jiley takes out her cell phone.

GRENDEL. Can't use that in here.
JILEY. What?
GRENDEL. Interferes with high-tech medical equipment. You might have just stopped some old lady's heart from beating.
JILEY. Oh my God. That's awful.
GRENDEL. Actually, you'd have to be right in the room with her. Don't worry, she's still suffering and alive. But it is a rule.
JILEY. OK. Well. Thank you.
GRENDEL. First time?
JILEY. Yes.
GRENDEL. What're you in for?
JILEY. Just a few tests.
GRENDEL. Well, I hope you pass.
JILEY. It's nothing.
GRENDEL. Oh, I'm sure they'll find something. Well, none of us comes out alive, right?
JILEY. Uh. True. But not. Anyway. Uh have a good morning.
GRENDEL. Not likely, I'd say. The morning is not likely to be good. Might as well just lie down and not get up, know what I mean? *(Jiley starts to do some stretches.)* I was thinking of taking some karate or judo. You ever study any of that self-defense?
JILEY. No. *(Jiley takes off her shoes.)*
GRENDEL. Wouldn't do that if I were you. Hospital's full of those antibiotic-resistant super germs. Don't want to get one of those on your feet. Only safe place around here is the bed. *(Jiley stops taking off her shoes, then picks up the phone near the bed.)* Oh, phone won't work. The monster in billing you just spent an hour

with? She's checking your credit record back to 1966, then maybe she'll turn it on. Next week. *(She opens the curtain.)* Curtain's completely transparent. Ridiculous, isn't it? Put in a curtain and make it transparent. Just like a hospital. You can use mine.
JILEY. That's OK.
GRENDEL. Jiley, right? Jiley Nance?
JILEY. Uh yeah.
GRENDEL. I saw it on the door.
JILEY. Oh. *(She looks, and her name is on the door.)*
GRENDEL. I know how you feel, I wouldn't want me for a neighbor either. Don't worry, I'm not dangerous, just cranky. Lonely. Been in here forever. Disease of unknown origin. Usually diagnosed at autopsy, they say. Don't worry, it's not contagious.
JILEY. Oh. I'm sorry.
GRENDEL. You're a kinda famous actress, aren't you?
JILEY. Oh, thanks. People don't usually know me. I mean, sometimes if they already know me, they'll know me.
GRENDEL. I looked you up on the Internet.
JILEY. Wow.
GRENDEL. Not much to do around here. You're the voice of the New York *Times*, right?
JILEY. You really did look me up.
GRENDEL. "To cancel delivery, press three." "To restart delivery, press two."
JILEY. Well, I *was* the voice. Now it's Maya Angelou.
GRENDEL. Oh, that's too bad. I'm sure *she* needed the job.
JILEY. No kidding.
GRENDEL. Life stinks, huh?
JILEY. I guess it can.
GRENDEL. But I read about that award you won.
JILEY. Oh, well. Yeah.
GRENDEL. It was a big deal, an up-and-coming kind of a thing. When was that?
JILEY. Oh, few years ago.
GRENDEL. Over ten, wasn't it?
JILEY. Well, yes, but since then I've —
GRENDEL. They said you had great promise. Great potential. Great things were expected of you. You were doing very well when you were mmm twenty-something. And you've had what, a moderate amount of success since then? In your limited field? What was that last job you had? The voice of maxi pads with wings? And your

one-woman show. Did that ever get produced? Have you been in any big movies lately? Or on Broadway? Off-Broadway? This decade? I know, it's hard. You're smart, talented, funny, attractive; you sing, you act, you write, no wonder you're not a household name.
JILEY. You got all that on the Internet?
GRENDEL. Single, aren't you? Never married. Your last long-term relationship was how many years ago? Five? Seven? Ten? And no kids, right? And how old are you?
JILEY. What did you say your name was?
GRENDEL. I didn't, but it's Lednerg.
JILEY. Lednerg?
GRENDEL. L-e-d-n-e-r-g.
JILEY. Have we met before?
GRENDEL. I don't know, have we?
JILEY. There's something familiar about you.
GRENDEL. How 'bout some music? *(Grendel puts on music. Something like Peggy Lee singing "Is That All There Is?"*)*
JILEY. Could you turn that down? *(Grendel turns it off. Jiley starts to unpack.)* Just for the record, I may have lost the *Times*, but I'm still the voice of Lifetime Television, *and* I'm doing an independent film that, OK, pays almost nothing, but it's well written, *and* I host a comedy show once a month, that OK, pays absolutely nothing, and perhaps you don't know much about show business, but as a woman, over a certain age, and over a certain height, not to mention, I'm not exactly blonde and blue-eyed, which all in all means I'm a little hard to cast. And it's not that I'm angry, 'cause I'm not. 'Cause I don't want to live my life being angry and hurting people's feelings by saying cruel and nasty things to them especially if I don't even know them, so I don't! Besides, I have a very nice boyfriend. *(Jiley takes out a photograph of her boyfriend.)*
GRENDEL. Oh, I'm sorry. Just trying to make conversation. My mistake. Got my facts wrong. Blame the yo-yos at Yahoo. *(Jiley's phone rings.)* See, the phone's working. What do I know?
JILEY. *(On phone.)* Oh, hi Sue, I'm glad you found me. *(She gets out her date book.)* Yes, I'm fine, just a little hypochondriacal. Tell them I'll be in the studio on Monday. What do you mean they don't want a woman to be the voice of Lifetime Television for Women anymore? Why not? Women prefer to listen to men? Since when? I'm not taking it personally. OK maybe I am. Well, that was different. No, I have nothing against Maya Angelou. I like Maya

* See Special Note on Songs and Recordings on copyright page.

Angelou. I I I do know why the caged bird sings! *(She slams the phone down. She tries to make a call, the phone doesn't work.)*
GRENDEL. Go ahead and use the cell, hon, I won't tell. Here, have some privacy. *(She closes the curtain. Jiley uses her cell, while Grendel boils water.)*
JILEY. Oh, Todd, hi. You won't believe what just happened with Sue — Oh. I understand. You were together for eight years, you have to give it another try. Again. No, I don't think you should call me if it doesn't work out, Todd. I mean I'm sure it will. She sounds selfish and psycho and spiteful, just like you, so I'm sure you'll have a happy life together — torturing each other! *(She hangs up. Cries. Grendel opens the curtain.)*
GRENDEL. Oh, tough day, huh? First your job, then your Todd. How 'bout a chocolate? *(Jiley nods. Grendel comes over and gives her one.)* Here, the dark kind. The bittersweet. *(Jiley takes it, cries more.)* Let's put you to bed, hon. Comes a time throwing in the towel is the best thing. I mean what's a towel for, if not to throw it in. *(Jiley gets in bed.)* Have some tea. It'll relax you. *(Grendel gives her tea, she drinks it, gets very woozy. Grendel straps Jiley into bed with straps that were hidden.)* I'll tuck you in. That's better, isn't it? I mean what do you have to look forward to? Menopause? Shrinking a couple of inches with age? A house in Weehawken?
JILEY. That's not so bad.
GRENDEL. Have another sip. After all, what have you done with your life? Convinced millions of unhappy women to watch television? And now that Todd is gone, who's left?
JILEY. Well.
GRENDEL. Besides your therapist.
JILEY. Well.
GRENDEL. Are you in love with anyone?
JILEY. Well.
GRENDEL. Who's also in love with you?
JILEY. Well.
GRENDEL. Is your best friend and confidante your pet?
JILEY. I love Tabby; she keeps me warm at night.
GRENDEL. The second half looks a lot worse than the first, and the first was quite a disappointment, wasn't it?
JILEY. How do you know?
GRENDEL. Believe me, there are a lot out there like you. Female, forty, formerly known as having potential, now known as that woman who loves her cat.

JILEY. Tabby isn't a cat, she's a turtle! Hey, what kind of drink is this?
GRENDEL. Special recipe. End-of-your-rope tea. *(She holds up the end of a rope.)*
JILEY. Wait a minute. I think —
GRENDEL. Don't bother to think, dear.
JILEY. I remember you now.
GRENDEL. Why don't you close your eyes.
JILEY. You're that voice.
GRENDEL. You're just confused.
JILEY. The one that makes me want to call my awful old boyfriend.
GRENDEL. Which awful old boyfriend?
JILEY. The voice that says I should go back to school and get a degree in midwifery.
GRENDEL. You think your current line of work is socially relevant?
JILEY. That hates it when the bus stops for the handicapped!
GRENDEL. Everyone hates that! *(Jiley starts to struggle out of the straps, while Grendel, across the room, prepares for a meal with a tablecloth, napkin, etc …)*
JILEY. You're the one who thinks the most I can achieve is slightly less than my mother. *(Grendel pulls out large salt and pepper shakers.)* And the most I can expect from a man is someone who'll call me to complain!
GRENDEL. Well? *(She gets out the meat tenderizer.)*
JILEY. You put fluorescent lights in bathrooms. And make me subscribe to *American Theatre* and read the *Arts and Leisure*.
GRENDEL. When were *you* last written up?
JILEY. We first met when I turned twelve. You told me to hate my hair and my height and my appetite. Lednerg. You're not Lednerg. *(Jiley is out of bed.)* You're Lednerg spelled backwards.
GRENDEL. No one will answer your call.
JILEY. You're … Grendel, the medieval monster. The eater of humans. *(Grendel throws off her hospital garb, and reveals her true sea monster self. She grabs a giant knife and fork and goes after Jiley. They fight. Grendel is much stronger.)*
GRENDEL. Face it, Jiley, you're no match for me. For every hope you hope, I bring out despair. For every dream you dream, I know not to care. And any time you think you're blessed, I cry: meaningless. Every time you're struck with love, I make sure you fuck it up.
JILEY. Now that I see you for what you are, I'll fight back.
GRENDEL. You don't have a chance! *(They fight. Jiley, much to*

Grendel's surprise, is getting stronger)

JILEY. We'll see about that! I may be middle-aged but you're from the Middle Ages, and I have an inner wolf that can bay, so Beowulf has nothing on me! *(They fight.)*

GRENDEL. I thought you never studied self-defense.

JILEY. I haven't. But I have had three years of stage combat! *(With a flourish, Jiley pins Grendel, and is about to finish her off.)*

GRENDEL. Jiley, you can't kill me.

JILEY. Why not?

GRENDEL. Think how much I've taught you. What was all that goddamn therapy about? Put our energies together and see how individuated you can be!

JILEY. Hmm. *(Jiley steps aside. Grendel gets away and grabs her weapons.)*

GRENDEL. You're stupider than I thought!

JILEY. Darn.

GRENDEL. Now I've got my spear of hopelessness *and* my sword soaked in cynicism. You can kiss your miserable life goodbye. You're about to become breakfast! *(Jiley scrambles for another weapon, but only comes up with a pen.)* Ha! What are you gonna fight me with — a pen?!

JILEY. What else?! *(They fight. Jiley somehow disarms Grendel then pins her with the pen.)* Goodbye Grendel! Once and for all! *(Jiley stabs Grendel with her pen.)*

GRENDEL. *(Dying)* Eeew. It's not over! Wait 'til you meet my mother!

JILEY. What's her name?

GRENDEL. She doesn't have one, just Grendel's mother.

JILEY. I don't think she'll be a problem; I've had a lot of practice with my own. *(Grendel dies. Jiley fixes herself up, looks in the mirror, is pleased, picks up her bag, grabs Grendel's spear and sword, starts to exit, then comes back, puts the weapons next to Grendel, tosses the photograph of Todd onto her body, and leaves. Grendel, using her sword and her spear, manages to pull herself up, looks out towards the audience. And smiles.)*

End of Play

PROPERTY LIST

Bones (GRENDEL)
Bucket (GRENDEL)
Overnight bag (JILEY)
Cell phone (JILEY)
Land-line phone (JILEY)
Various clothing (JILEY)
Photograph (JILEY)
Date book (JILEY)
Pot of water (GRENDEL)
Chocolate (GRENDEL)
Cup of tea (GRENDEL)
Rope (GRENDEL)
Tablecloth (GRENDEL)
Napkin (GRENDEL)
Salt and pepper shakers (GRENDEL)
Meat tenderizer (GRENDEL)
Giant knife and fork (GRENDEL)
Pen (JILEY)
Mirror (JILEY)

SOUND EFFECTS

Phone ringing

CREATIVE DEVELOPMENT

Creative Development was first produced by the Shadowbox Theatre in Columbus, Ohio.

CHARACTERS

DOUG BELLOWS, 65. The creative director for an important film company. Animated, intense, volatile.

DIANE ISIS, 25. Posing as a playwright, really a goddess. Bright, sharp, strong.

THE MUSES, nine women of all shapes and sizes.

PLACE

Here.

TIME

Now.

NOTE: Feel free to change/update the movie references at the end of the play.

CREATIVE DEVELOPMENT

A nice office. Plastic palm tree. Doug Bellows sits at his desk. He picks up a piece of paper, looks at it for a second, puts it down. A woman enters. She wears a coat.

DOUG. Hello, hello. Come in, come in.
DIANE. Hi.
DOUG. Have a seat. Nice to meet you.
DIANE. Thank you for calling.
DOUG. Always like to meet young writers. Take off your coat.
DIANE. That's OK.
DOUG. You cold? *(She nods.)* Damn, I'm sweating up a storm up here. Water? *(He opens a bottle of water; she pulls a glass out of her bag.)*
DIANE. Thank you.
DOUG. Well. Hmm. *(He pours some water into her glass. They drink.)* So uh uh *(He looks at his paper.),* Dierdre.
DIANE. Donna.
DOUG. Yes. I'm Doug.
DIANE. Right.
DOUG. Bellows.
DIANE. Yes.
DOUG. Let's be frank, Donna, your play is not a movie.
DIANE. Oh?
DOUG. No, your play, I'm afraid, is definitely a play. And a play is almost never going to be a movie.
DIANE. Well, I thought —
DOUG. Now I didn't actually see your play.
DIANE. Oh?
DOUG. Oh, I tried, but it was raining, dear.
DIANE. Uh huh.
DOUG. Do you know what it's like to get a cab in the rain? It's hell.
DIANE. Maybe you could come another night.

DOUG. I thought it was over. *(He looks at his paper.)*
DIANE. It's been extended.
DOUG. Oh, well. How did that happen?
DIANE. Word of mouth, people liking it, that sort of thing.
DOUG. I see. Well, I'm sure it'll close soon, don't you think?
DIANE. No, actually I'm hoping it'll run for a very long time.
DOUG. Ha ha ha, I doubt that.
DIANE. I'd be happy to get you tickets.
DOUG. It's my wife, she can't make it.
DIANE. Maybe you could come without her. *(She pulls a ticket out of her bag.)*
DOUG. Now, Donna, the point is, regardless, it's not a movie. I've read the coverage. *(He holds the paper over his head, he chuckles.)* And it's not a movie. I mean what does it have? Live people talking to each other? Ha. Now, is there anyone famous in it?
DIANE. No.
DOUG. I know this may be hard to hear, and you seem like a particularly lovely young person. See, I used to be in the theatre, I was an actor once, a very good one, very, you know, good, and well I gave it up and I'm much better off now. It's really a pleasure to meet you. Sure you won't take off that coat? *(She shakes her head no.)* Can I get you anything? Cappuccino?
DIANE. Thank you, I have my own. *(She pulls a cappuccino out of her bag.)*
DOUG. Hmm. So. Uh *(He presses his buzzer.)*, cappuccino, one. Donna, now. Hmm, I'm sure your play was nice, very uh interesting, but I bet it didn't pay the rent, did it, and how many people actually saw it, right? I know you wouldn't be here if you weren't interested in writing movies. Everyone wants to go to the movies, and everyone wants to do movies. It's well, something magical. *(A hand appears in the doorway holding a cappuccino. He retrieves it. Diane offers him a shaker of cinnamon from her bag.)*
DOUG. Uh. Thanks.
DIANE. Mr. Bellows.
DOUG. Doug, please.
DIANE. Doug, you have some foam. On your mouth.
DOUG. Oh. Thank you. So you gotta understand the hell we're in here. The people I work for are big powerful people, and they want big powerful movies. High concept. Now your play, if we made it into a movie, which we never would, would be an art film, and no one wants an art film and if they say they do they're a big

fat liar. Ha! Let me introduce you to someone. *(He presses a buzzer.)* Send in Stew. I'm gonna do you a big favor. *(A door opens. Stew's shadow is seen.)*

DOUG. Stew, this is a writer, a playwright. *(Stew leaves.)* Never turn down a meeting, that's how things happen. So, where was I?

DIANE. My play.

DOUG. Right. By the way, how did you get it produced?

DIANE. Excuse me?

DOUG. How did you get that theatre to do your play? What exactly did you have to do?

DIANE. I think they liked it.

DOUG. Really? Huh. See I used to be in the theatre, I was a director, did some very interesting, you know, unusual nonliterary, I mean nonlinear work, maybe you know of it. Anyway, now I'm lucky enough to be here and help out playwrights like yourself. 'Cause I can tell by the cut of your coat I make a pretty penny more than you, dear. Would you like to read some screenplays? We have quite a collection.

DIANE. Have you produced any of them?

DOUG. What?

DIANE. What movies have you actually produced here?

DOUG. Donna! Are you with me?

DIANE. Yes.

DOUG. I'm going to tell you something very important now. About how to sell a movie. Are you listening?

DIANE. I'm listening.

DOUG. *(Clearly.)* The only way to make a movie is to make one that's already been made. You got it?

DIANE. Maybe you could say it again. A little louder.

DOUG. The only way to make a movie is to make one that's already been made! Like like Gump. *(He jumps up.) Gump.* Do you have a *Gump*? I gotta get a *Gump*.

DIANE . Um.

DOUG. *Gump*. I need a *Gump*. Do you have a *Gump Gump Gump*.

DIANE. Are you all right?

DOUG. Yes *Gump* I'm all right *Gump* of course I'm all right why wouldn't I be all right?

DIANE. I'm going to go out on a limb here and tell you it's very important that you see my play.

DOUG. What? What are you talking about?

DIANE. We could go right now.
DOUG. What?
DIANE. I strongly suggest it.
DOUG. No.
DIANE. How about another play?
DOUG. Excuse me?
DIANE. Why not?
DOUG. Look, I think I've made my point here. Are you interested in pitching or what? Do you have any big ideas? Like like —
DIANE. My play.
DOUG. You're not getting the message. Why are you not getting the message?
DIANE. Come to my play.
DOUG. No way.
DIANE. I'm warning you.
DOUG. You're warning me — very funny — the nerve. This is my office.
DIANE. What are you afraid of?
DOUG. Afraid? What do I have to be afraid of?
DIANE. Then why not?
DOUG. Because because I don't go to the theatre. All right? Why should I? No one goes. Who goes? Tourists? Other people in the theatre? It's pathetic, it's elitist, it's too expensive, you can't eat popcorn, you can't go to the bathroom 'til intermission, and nowadays a play doesn't even have an intersmisson. Does yours?
DIANE. No.
DOUG. See? I have a very small bladder. *(She hands him a plastic urine bottle from her bag. He grabs it and uses it for emphasis.)* Hell no I won't go. It's dying, it's dead. You know that. Everyone does. So give it up. Wake up. Donna!!! Wake up!! There is no theatre anymore, it's a dinosaur on its last fart. Who goes — no one! Stop with the plays start with the blockbusters. *Gump Gump Gump*! *(Very calm.)* So, I'm sure if you have something like like that movie I mentioned I'm sure we could work together, collaborate. Very nicely. Very successfully.
DIANE. Bellows.
DOUG. Yes?
DIANE. I'm not really a playwright.
DOUG. Thank God, I didn't think you were. You certainly don't act like one.
DIANE. My name isn't Donna.

DOUG. Oh?
DIANE. It's Diane. *(Thunder and lightning as she pulls off her coat, revealing a mini toga. She is a powerful goddess.)*
DIANE. Diane Isis. You just failed the last test.
DOUG. Very funny ha ha.
DIANE. I'm not kidding, Doug.
DOUG. Who put you up to this, Stew? That guy. *(He presses a buzzer.)*
DIANE. There is no more Stew.
DOUG. Yeah, right, good one.
DIANE . Do you hear that? *(She opens her bag. We hear lovely singing.)* Those are the muses, all nine of them, they've been listening to your every word, and they can't believe what they've heard.
DOUG. Oh, I'm shaking. What did I do?
DIANE. Impersonated a creative director.
DOUG. I am a creative director.
DIANE. Ha!
DOUG. Is this some kind of a pitch? A feminist *Gladiator* remake? Well, it's not working.
DIANE. Bellows! Did you think you could get away with it? Did you think no one was watching? Calling in thousands of playwrights to humiliate them, to convince them to stop writing plays and start writing movies?
DOUG. Now look Dierdre Donna Diane I have another meeting in a minute, so —
DIANE. You're telling writers what to do? Isn't that a little upside down, Doug? Shouldn't it really be the other way around, Doug? *(A ferocious wind blows. Doug holds onto his desk for dear life.)*
DOUG. What the hell was that?
DIANE. That was Calliope exhaling.
DOUG. OK OK, this meeting is over.
DIANE. This meeting has just begun!!!!
DOUG. What are you after? A deal? Well fine, let's hear it.
DIANE. Your deal days are done, Doug. You've turned the artistic world upside down and we're here to set it straight and the first casualty is you.
DOUG. Have we met before?
DIANE. You hear that? *(We hear hissing.)* Those are the sisters they're morphing into something a little more s-s-sinsiter.
DOUG. Hey, I'm just doing my job.
DIANE. We know all about your job, what you really do here. The

underground network, the anti-theatre lobbying effort, the *I Won't Go to the Theatre Newsletter*. And we are not amused. We know you've converted millions, and raised money into the billions. We know who you contributed to in the last election. We know all about you.

DOUG. I got nothing to hide. Maybe that was me, but I'm not killing the theatre, I'm protecting audiences all over the world from an intolerable night out. What are you gonna do? Fire me? Go ahead, there'll be someone else here tomorrow.

DIANE. Why'd you do it, Doug? Fear? Was that it? Afraid of seeing something that might make you uncomfortable? Well, you're about to learn the real meaning of the word. Sisters! *(From out of her bag emerge nine women of all shapes and sizes. They all wear mini togas with a large M on them, and have snakes in their hair.)*

DOUG. Well, uh hello, uh, ladies.

DIANE. Prepare for your final treatment. We have come for our revenge.

MUSES & DIANE. *(They roar at him.)* Rah! *(The lights change.)*

DOUG. Now hang on, let's be reasonable here. *(They surround him, and they tie him up.)*

MUSES. *(They roar.)* Rah!

DOUG. Now now look what are you doing? I mean, I get it, OK? You made your point. Hey! Please. I'm just human, right? I mean do you know how hard it is to make a living in the theatre? *(They pull out their weapons. One has a giant paintbrush, one has a musical instrument, one has a big pair of toe shoes, another a chisel. Diane pulls out a mirror. They start to create something.)*

DOUG. OK, what do you want? I'll let you make an art film, OK? You can make that Dierdre's play into a very arty art film. We can work together, do things from the inside. I know where you're coming from. I used to be in the theatre. I was a producer. Not for profit! *(The muses and Diane have created an instant stage for Doug.)*

DIANE. OK, Bellows. Create.

DOUG. What?

DIANE. You're in a theatre, you're on the stage.

DOUG. What?

DIANE. You've got an audience. *(House lights come up.)*

DOUG. Oh my God, I do.

DIANE. It's live. Create.

DOUG. I. I.

DIANE. Create!!! Write a poem, recite a play, do a dance. They're waiting.

DOUG. *(To audience.)* Uh. Hello. Uh. *(To Diane.)* OK, I'll call those playwrights. I'll call every playwright and apologize. Diane? Oh God, Diane? *(To audience.)* Ha ha ha. Uh. Uh. *(To Diane.)* I'll cancel the committee. I was wrong. I admit it. Diane? *(To audience.)* Uh uh. *(The muses as audience start to cough, unwrap candy wrappers, shuffle, and answer their ringing cell phones. To Diane.)* Think of my wife. My kids. I have daughters: one does modern dance, the other plays the piano, I swear. Uh … U … I can't. Please. I I can't. I'm not creative. I'm not. I have no ideas. None. None.

DIANE. This is your life now, Doug. For eternity this is what you will be: an actor/director/producer on stage without a play. Forever.

DOUG. Oh God. Look, OK, this is very hard for me, but I'll go to the play. I will, I'll go to that Donna's play. Please! Forgive me. My life is hell. You have to understand. I'm the one who turned down *Gump. (He sobs.)* It's true. For ten years I said no to *Gump.* And look what happened.

DIANE. Doug, wasn't that a very long time ago?

DOUG. Yes, but but I haven't beeen able to get past it.

MUSE 1. *(A young muse speaks.)* Wow.

MUSE 2. *(A large muse speaks.) Gump.*

MUSE 3. *(An old muse.)* That's bad.

MUSE 4. *(A dim muse.)* Really bad.

MUSE 5. *(A loud muse.)* Yeah.

MUSE 6. *(A silly muse.)* I can't believe he did that.

MUSE 7. *(A fast muse.)* Talk about stupid.

MUSE 8. *(A sloppy muse.)* Dumb.

MUSE 9. *(A muse like muse.)* Pathetic.

ALL MUSES. (All the muses.) Maybe he's suffered enough. *(They look to Diane, she thinks.)*

STAN. I have. Really. I have. and look, uh ladies, I mean we've come a long way since uh, the days of Homer and those other guys. We've developed, creatively. Right? I mean, compassion and all that, forgiveness. *(They look at each other.)* I said I'd go to the play. I mean isn't that the point? I mean. I will go. Why we can all go. I mean, have you seen that play? (*The muses look away, embarrassed.)* We can go together: you, me; man, uh women; the past, the present. Group rate. How's that? *(The lights brighten. A reprieve.)*

DIANE. Hmm. Untie him. *(They start to slowly untie him. Diane puts on her coat.)*

DOUG. Oh thank you, thank you. You won't regret it. From now

on I'll be different. I swear. Very different.
DIANE. Hmm, Doug.
DOUG. Yeah?
DIANE. Before we go —
DOUG. What is it, dear?
DIANE. I have this idea. For a movie. Blockbuster. I thought I'd just try it out on you.
DOUG. Oh?
DIANE. It's about a guy who dresses as a woman. An unattractive woman.
DOUG. It's been done.
DIANE. Exactly. There's a lot of biblical-type suffering.
DOUG. That's been done, sounds good.
DIANE. Takes place in wine country.
DOUG. I'm listening.
DIANE. It's animated and has an ugly duckling sort of theme.
DOUG. Go on.
DIANE. And the thing is … The main character, the one dressed as the very unattractive woman, he's also … dumb.
DOUG. Oh.
DIANE. Very dumb.
DOUG. Yeah?
DIANE. Stupid.
DOUG. Uh huh.
DIANE. And unattractive.
DOUG. I see.
DIANE. Ugly.
DOUG. Right.
DIANE. And we can call it …
DOUG. What? … What? What?
DIANE. We can call it … *Frump*.
DOUG. *FRUMP!* I love it! We'll make it.
DIANE. Tie him up!
MUSES. *(They roar.)* Rah! *(Diane throws off her coat, weapons come out. Blackout.)*

End of Play

PROPERTY LIST

Paper (DOUG)
Bottle of water (DOUG)
Glass (DOUG)
Ticket (DIANE)
2 cappucinos (DOUG, DIANE)
Shaker of cinnamon (DIANE)
Plastic urine bottle (DIANE)
Mirror (DIANE)
Rope (MUSES)
Giant paintbrush, musical instrument, big pair of toe shoes, chisel (MUSES)
Candy wrappers (MUSES)
Cell phones (MUSES)

SOUND EFFECTS

Buzzer
Thunder
Muses singing
Hissing
Roaring
Cell phones ringing

2B (OR NOT 2B)
PART 2

2B (OR NOT 2B) PART 2 was first performed in the HB Short Play Festival 2004 "The Wedding Plays" (William Carden, Artistic Director; Pamela Berlin, Playwrights Unit Director) in New York City. It was directed by Michael Barakiva. The set design was by David Korin; the costume design was by Maggie Lee-Burdoff; the lighting design was by Chris Dallos; the sound design was by Shane Rettig; the production manager was Matt Britt; and the production stage manager was Tiffany Tillman. The cast was as follows:

FRANNY .... Jeanine Serralles
PIANOBOY .... P.J. Sosko

CHARACTERS

FRANNY, 30s, a Queen bee. Used to be a human female.

PIANOBOY, a really cute musician.

PLACE

A tasteful wedding.

TIME

Now.

2B (OR NOT 2B) PART 2

A wedding. Cocktail hour before the reception. Lights up on Franny, a human-sized bee, wearing a tiara and holding a drink.

FRANNY. *(To the audience.)* I wasn't always a bee, I used to be a female human of a certain age with a certain career, but after Frank left me for Eleanor, a human female still fertile, I ran away with Dave, a large drone who recruited me to be the Queen by promising free room and board, all the hot sex I wanted with as many drones as I liked, and the diamond tiara I now wear on my head. That human, Frank, broke my heart in a million pieces and ruined my life in a million ways. Not that I blame him. 'Cause I don't. I know you're not supposed to. It's pathetic, it's unfeminist, it's the goddamn truth. When he told me the most despicable things about his sorry life and threatened suicide, I gave him a lovely package of bath products, wrote out the number for the suicide hotline, and told him I would never leave. So he left me. For Eleanor, my former friend with a Ph.D. in semiotic videography who once dated one of the Baldwin brothers I forget which one, but he wasn't cute. When I told Frank that Eleanor had the papilloma virus in her mouth and her *vagina,* he thought I was lying, which I was, and stopped returning my calls. So when Dave, a strappingly handsome drone, came to my door and lured me with his luring talk, I converted. Entomologically. And being a bee is a helluva lot better than being a human female of a certain age and a certain career. Did you know that the young female worker bees are all sexually undeveloped? That the Queen is the only one who gets any? I've got the whole hive after my tail. I am their fucking Queen. Constantly. So when I heard through the grapevine — literally — that Frank and Eleanor were getting married, I thought I'd come by, make peace, and leave a jar of honey … laced with arsenic. Just kidding. I wouldn't do that. I've softened. I've rounded. I've changed — species. I help cross-pollinate now allowing fruit trees to flower, almonds to bud, and bleeding hearts to blossom. So I put on my dress wings, polished my crown, and caught the nearest tailwind to get here. I'll applaud the happy couple, say congratulations, then stick my stinger right up his married ass. 'Cause he's allergic, and he'll die! I've moved on from anger. Right into rage and revenge. Look at this. Even the flowers are tasteful, and I know flowers. And the music, perfect. They must have spent a fortune. I helped Frank get his ridiculously high-paying job and now he's rich, married, and I'm. A fat bee. I haven't heard music since I left humanity. All I've done is fuck drones. And catch up on old *New Yorkers*. Suck pollen. Not that I'm bitter. I'm sweet. Because I'm so filled with honey if you poked me I'd splat. I'm gonna shoot my poison into Frank's happy heart and halt its harmonious beating for good. I'll fuck it all up. Then leave mankind forever. Leave men forever. What is that music?! *(She yells towards the piano player.)* Hey, Music Guy cut it out! I might have to kill him, too. Hey Pianoboy! *(She freezes, stunned. To audience.)* OHMYGOD! He is so cute! *(Pianoboy enters.)*

PIANOBOY. What's going on?

FRANNY. What is your problem playing music like that? I'm working up a maniacal rage.

PIANOBOY. Nice outfit.

FRANNY. Don't nice outfit me.

PIANOBOY. Your stripes too tight or something?

FRANNY. Don't bug me.

PIANOBOY. Would you like another drink?

FRANNY. You're probably gonna go hit on the girlfriends of the bride who feel like shit their friend is getting married but have to pretend they're happy. Look at them trying to attract your attention in their ridiculously short skirts and pathetically high heels.

PIANOBOY. It's a beautiful thing.

FRANNY. You probably think foreplay is to get a woman to stop thinking about her next pair of shoes.

PIANOBOY. Now that you mention it.

FRANNY. Buzz off.

PIANOBOY. Hey, you talked to me.

FRANNY. Just 'cause you're impossibly cute doesn't mean I'm attracted to you. I'm not even a human anymore.

PIANOBOY. I noticed.

FRANNY. I'm a bee. And I get plenty. I have no problem getting any. As a bee. I'm busy. As a bee. *(He sings a verse from a song like*

"Honeysuckle Rose.")* I can't imagine doing it with a human again —
PIANOBOY. Bee sex. How does that work?
FRANNY. — All those — limbs.
PIANOBOY. You get turned on by roundness of the shape?
FRANNY. And that — slippery skin.
PIANOBOY. Or the delicacy of the wing?
FRANNY. Women must jump all over you.
PIANOBOY. The taste of the royal jelly.
FRANNY. Those eyes. Those full lips.
PIANOBOY. The bend in your antennae.
FRANNY. That hair.
PIANOBOY. Your nectar.
FRANNY. Those peasant feet.
PIANOBOY. That buzz.
FRANNY. Your voice.
PIANOBOY. The way you fly.
FRANNY. The bulge in your fly. *(They jump on each other. Under the gift table.)* Just watch out for my stinger.
PIANOBOY. Watch out for mine! *(Their legs and arms stick out from under the table. Much activity.)*

FRANNY	PIANOBOY.
Buzz! Buzz! Oh!	Oh! Oh! Buzz!

(They emerge.)
FRANNY. Wow, that was — *(She grabs him. They go at it again.)*

FRANNY	PIANOBOY.
Oh! Oh! Buzz!	Buzz! Buzz! Oh!

(They emerge.)
FRANNY. Ohmygod that was great that was warm soft hard close intimate exquisite —
PIANOBOY. Yeah. Bee sex is hot.
FRANNY. I never knew it could feel like that. How did you do that?
PIANOBOY. I am all over your fuzz.
FRANNY. Skin sweat lips fingers. I haven't had fingers for forever.
PIANOBOY. What does a queen bee do all day anyway?
FRANNY. Pretty much fuck all the time.
PIANOBOY. You got it going on.
FRANNY. How am I gonna go back to drones?
PIANOBOY. How am I gonna go back to twenty-year olds?
FRANNY. I long for you. I ache. I want to eat pastrami sandwiches

* See Special Note on Songs and Recordings on copyright page.

chocolate ice cream, and sleep on a mattress together. I want to know all about you.
PIANOBOY. I like beer.
FRANNY. I like your knee joints your fatless butt and the fact that you walk don't fly.
PIANOBOY. Let's go to bars and make out.
FRANNY. Buy me a present.
PIANOBOY. How 'bout a piece of chocolate cake?
FRANNY. You have the best face I've ever seen.
PIANOBOY. You have great … bee boobies.
FRANNY. Are you seeing other women?
PIANOBOY. Not since we met.
FRANNY. My favorite playwright is Caryl Churchill.
PIANOBOY. My favorite monkey is the bonobo.
FRANNY. I love bonobos! Matriarchal society.
PIANOBOY. Yeah. Like how they fuck all the time instead of fighting. I'm like that.
FRANNY. You are!?
PIANOBOY. Can I get your number? Maybe you could come over and we could you know get under the kitchen table.
FRANNY. You want my number!? It's — oh no I don't have a number! *(Sobs hysterically.)* I can't believe I finally meet a guy I like and I'm a bee!
PIANOBOY. Wow. That's a problem.
FRANNY. I can't be a human again. I'm irreversible!
PIANOBOY. I can't be a bee. I don't really like bees.
FRANNY. And I don't really like men.
PIANOBOY. I need a drink. You want something?
FRANNY. So now you're gonna leave? You're just gonna walk out and leave? Hit the road, put on your coat, take your marbles, your nasal spray, your scotch, and boogie woogie back to your books your mountain bike your butterfly-catching kit?
PIANOBOY. I don't have any of those things. Well, I have a bike but —
FRANNY. I know you! You don't call or you call too much or you only call late at night.
PIANOBOY. I don't even have your number.
FRANNY. You're sweet only then to be cruel. You promise me a rose garden then refuse to buy me flowers.
PIANOBOY. I was just gonna get a beer. You want some wine?
FRANNY. If you're so smart why can't you understand that leaving

at six A.M. with barely a word will hurt my feelings? And when you do stay, why do you wake me up by shouting, "Hey, get up"?

PIANOBOY. Who are you talking about?

FRANNY. You're gonna pack your port, and go back to your wife, your girlfriend, your dog, your big house, your little apartment, your cabin, your villa, your kids, your antiques, your coffee plunger, your three-car garage, and your multiple sunglasses. When you said you were separated I thought it meant legally not physically. When you said you wanted children, I thought it meant with me. When you said you'd never leave I thought it meant — you'd never leave! You came into my life, defrosted the tundra of my heart and now I'll never hear from you again? I wait up for your calls I want your emails I send you erotic letters you don't answer —

PIANOBOY. We just met —

FRANNY. And it feels like forever! I can't believe after everything I've been through I'm here again. Hoping that you'll love me or like me or at least want to have sex with me on a semi-regular basis. I love you I don't know how to live without you. Oh no! I'm feeling like a human female of a certain age and a certain career! No! NO! NO!

PIANOBOY. Hey hey hey, it's me, Pianoboy. I'm the only one here. Right? I'm your monkeyman who made you feel all good under the table. That's all I'm doing, right? I'm not those other guys. It's me — Bonoboboy. Come on. *(He kisses her.)* Hey, baby, honeypie, I don't even know your name.

FRANNY. It's Francesca. But you can call me Franny.

PIANOBOY. I'm Emanuel, but you can call me Manny.

FRANNY. Manny?

MANNY. Franny?

FRANNY. Manny?

MANNY. Franny?

FRANNY. Would you really have called?

MANNY. Sure.

FRANNY. How often?

MANNY. Couple times a week.

FRANNY. For how long?

MANNY. A while.

FRANNY. And then?

MANNY. Once a week. Every other week. Once a month. Maybe.

FRANNY. I'm so glad I'm not a human.

MANNY. I'm so glad I'm not married. That poor guy.

FRANNY. Frank!

MANNY. Yeah, the groom.
FRANNY. I completely forgot. I came here to kill him.
MANNY. Glad I got paid upfront.
FRANNY. All I wanted was for him to suffer.
MANNY. He's married, that'll take care of itself.
FRANNY. But now. I couldn't care less. I mean I still hope he has a short painful horrible life filled with suffering, misery, and hardship, but other than that I don't care. I haven't thought about him since we met. You changed my life.
MANNY. And you opened me up to a whole new world of insect copulation.
FRANNY. Manny, we can't stay together. The Bee/Human thing only leads to heartache. It's best if I go.
MANNY. You mean? Back to the hive?
FRANNY. God no, those drones wear me out.
MANNY. Other pastures?
FRANNY. Flying solo. You?
MANNY. I'm grooving.
FRANNY. You're a beautiful man.
MANNY. And you're a rockin, Queen. How 'bout a —
FRANNY. — goodbye kiss? *(They kiss. It's hot.)*
MANNY. Gimme a squeeze. *(She squeezes him. Hard.)* Whoa! How bout we —
FRANNY. — go to your place? Just for tonight.
MANNY. I'm good with that.
FRANNY. Me too. I'll buzz off in the morning.
MANNY. I'll make you fuzzy buzzy 'til then.
FRANNY. I'm feeling fuzzy buzzy right now. Can we go?
MANNY. I still have to play for — forget it. Let's get a cab.
FRANNY. No need. Just get on my back and we'll fly.
MANNY. I got the keyboard, the amp, the mic —
FRANNY. Hop on. I can carry you. All of you. Come on, Pianoboy. *(He gets on her back.)* Let's fly. *(Spotlight on them. Singing. Flying.)*

End of Play

PROPERTY LIST

Tiara (FRANNY)
Drink (FRANNY)

SOUND EFFECTS

Piano music

TUNNEL OF LOVE

TUNNEL OF LOVE was first performed in the 1993 Issues Project at Naked Angels (Jennifer Estess, Producer) in New York City. It was directed by Ethan Silverman. The cast was as follows:

SUSIE .... Martha Plimpton
GARY .... Merrill Holtzman
ENSEMBLE .... Kimberly Flynn
ENSEMBLE .... Susan Greenhill
ENSEMBLE .... Karen Kandel

TUNNEL OF LOVE was first fully produced at The Ensemble Studio Theatre (Curt Dempster, Artistic Director) in their 1993 Marathon in New York City. It was directed by Ethan Silverman. The cast was as follows:

SUSIE .... Amelia Campbell
GARY .... David Eigenberg
ENSEMBLE .... Bill Cwikowski
ENSEMBLE .... Christine Farrell
ENSEMBLE .... Karen Kandel
ENSEMBLE .... Angela Pietropinto

TUNNEL OF LOVE was produced in 1996 in Los Angeles by Theatre of Note. It received a Drama-Logue Award in Playwriting.

CHARACTERS

SUSIE, quirky, confused, trying to cope as the world spins around her. In her early 20s.

GARY, a guy's guy. Trying hard to do his best. In his 20s.

DOCTOR CHECKUP

DOCTOR MUFFIN

DOCTOR BEAVER

DOCTOR SNATCH

DOCTOR TOO-LIPS

JO

FIFI

THERESA

WOMAN 1

WOMAN 2

WOMAN 3

WOMAN 4

TIME

Now.

NOTE: An ensemble of three to four actors should play all roles except Susie and Gary. It should include actors of all shapes, sizes, ethnicities, ages; men can play women, women can play men, etc. … Also, there are no blackouts between scenes.

TUNNEL OF LOVE

Scene 1

Doctor's office. Susie sits in a tiny child-sized chair. Doctor Checkup sits in a large chair. He looks very big. On his chest is a name tag that reads, "Dr. Anton Checkup." He has a Russian accent.

DOCTOR CHECKUP. So. I'm Dr. Anton Checkup. And you're — *(He looks at a paper.)* Susie. So. Any aches and pains?
SUSIE. No.
DOCTOR CHECKUP. Ongoing childhood diseases?
SUSIE. No.
DOCTOR CHECKUP. Shortness of breath?
SUSIE. No.
DOCTOR CHECKUP. Runny nose?
SUSIE. No.
DOCTOR CHECKUP. Post-feminist depression?
SUSIE. No.
DOCTOR CHECKUP. Tummy ache?
SUSIE. No.
DOCTOR CHECKUP. Heartache?
SUSIE. Um, well, no.
DOCTOR CHECKUP. Problems with peeing or pooping?
SUSIE. No.
DOCTOR CHECKUP. Exercise.
SUSIE. StairMaster.
DOCTOR CHECKUP. Ulcer due to backlash anger?
SUSIE. No.
DOCTOR CHECKUP. Eyes? *(Susie points to her eyes.)* Ears? *(She points to ears.)* Nose? *(She points to nose.)*
DOCTOR CHECKUP. Married?
SUSIE. No.

DOCTOR CHECKUP. In a relationship?
SUSIE. Uh, no. I was, but he um, just left me.
DOCTOR CHECKUP. *(He looks at her.)* Anorgasmic or orgasmic?
SUSIE. Excuse me?
DOCTOR CHECKUP. Have you had one or haven't you?
SUSIE. Umm.
DOCTOR CHECKUP. Hmm. And no trouble peeing or pooping.
SUSIE. No.
DOCTOR CHECKUP. My wife's a social worker, I recommend counseling. Otherwise, you're healthy. Come back next year. Find a man. Pay 600 dollar bill at desk.
SUSIE. Wait.
DOCTOR CHECKUP. Yes?
SUSIE. I do have a problem.
DOCTOR CHECKUP. Yes.
SUSIE. With.
DOCTOR CHECKUP. Yes?
SUSIE. My.
DOCTOR CHECKUP. Yes? *(She crosses to him and stands on tiptoe to whisper in his ear.)* Oh. Go on. *(She whispers.)* Interesting. I'd like to have a look at that.

Scene 2

Phone call. Gary in his apartment, fixing something with his tools. Susie at home.

SUSIE. Gary?
GARY. Yeah?
SUSIE. Hi, it's Susie.
GARY. Oh, hi. Hang on. *(He uses his screwdriver.)*
SUSIE. What are you doing?
GARY. Fixing objects so that I can feel like I have infinite power over my world.
SUSIE. Nice.
GARY. Sorry things didn't work out with us. I just couldn't handle it. I mean. I still can't. I mean, let's cut to the chase here. Why

are you calling?
SUSIE. I just wanted to say that — *(He drops something.)* What are you doing?
GARY. Breaking things so that I can fix them so that I can feel like I have infinite power over my world.
SUSIE. Oh. Well, I went to the doctor.
GARY. Good. It's good to take action.
SUSIE. You were right.
GARY. It's good to be right. Tough break for you, though.
SUSIE. Well, the doctor said there was hope.
GARY. Oh? You mean like a repair job?
SUSIE. And I was wondering, if they can, you know —
GARY. I see — would I want to be a couple — movies, dinner, nesting, that sort of thing.
SUSIE. The doctor recommended it.
GARY. Look, uh, my my phone is ringing.
SUSIE. It is?
GARY. I mean, the door is ringing.
SUSIE. I have an appointment with a specialist.
GARY. Hey, well, like, I don't know, I mean, yours seemed like a problem even I couldn't fix. So, let me know what happens, if you get it worked out or worked in or whatever. Susie. You're a sweetheart. Gotta go. *(He exits.)*

Scene 3

Another doctor's office. Susie sits on her little chair, or on a table with wheels. Doctor appears.

DOCTOR MUFFIN. I'm Dr. Muffin.
SUSIE. Hi, Dr. Checkup gave me your name. I was —
DOCTOR MUFFIN. Oh, yes. Mind if I take a look? *(Susie spreads her legs. Doctor Beaver appears.)*
DOCTOR BEAVER. I'm Dr. Beaver.
DOCTOR MUFFIN. Interesting.
SUSIE. Hi, Dr. Muffin gave me your name. I was wondering —
DOCTOR BEAVER. Interesting. Mind if I take a look? *(Doctor*

Snatch appears.)
DOCTOR SNATCH. I'm Dr. Snatch.
SUSIE. Dr. um, Beaver gave me your name. I was wondering if —
DOCTOR MUFFIN. So, you growing potatoes in there?
SUSIE. What?
DOCTOR BEAVER. Are you married?
SUSIE. No.
DOCTOR SNATCH. Oh, yes, mind if I —
SUSIE. — take a look?
DOCTOR BEAVER. In a relationship?
DOCTOR MUFFIN. Post-feminist depression?
SUSIE. Ooh.
DOCTOR SNATCH. Interesting.
DOCTOR BEAVER. Are you seeing a psychiatrist?
SUSIE. Ow.
DOCTOR MUFFIN. Do you mind it when men sit with their legs spread apart?
DOCTOR BEAVER. My cousin's an analyst.
DOCTOR SNATCH. I'd like to take a look.
DOCTOR MUFFIN. I like to look.
SUSIE. Doctor, do you think — ?
DOCTOR MUFFIN. Let me call in my partners. *(Doctor Too-Lips appears.)*
DOCTOR TOO-LIPS. I'm Dr. Too-Lips.
DOCTOR BEAVER. Get the camera.
SUSIE. Hey. *(Susie is spun around and/or pulled around the stage. Or perhaps it's just the doctors that are moving. At some point, strange, large examining instruments appear.)*
DOCTOR MUFFIN. I think there's someone else I'd like you to see.
DOCTOR TOO-LIPS. Do you have a boyfriend?
DOCTOR BEAVER. I think I'd like to see.
DOCTOR TOO-LIPS. Do you have a friend?
DOCTOR SNATCH. I'd like you to come back.
DOCTOR BEAVER. We think it can be fixed.
DOCTOR TOO-LIPS. Do you know any men?
SUSIE. Hey!
DOCTOR MUFFIN. Interesting.
DOCTOR SNATCH. I can't see.
DOCTOR BEAVER. Let me look.
DOCTOR TOO-LIPS. I'd like to see. *(Doctors in a circle around Susie, passing the instruments to each other. Fast:)*

DR. MUFFIN	DR. BEAVER	DR. SNATCH	DR. TOO-LIPS
I can't see.	Let me look.	Interesting.	Do you have a
Interesting.	I'd like to see.	I can't see.	boyfriend? Do
I can't see.	Let me look.	Interesting.	you have a
Interesting.	I'd like to see.	I can't see.	friend? Do you
I can't see.	Let me look.	Interesting.	have a boy-
Interesting.	I'd like to see.	I can't see.	friend? Do you?

DOCTORS. *I'd like to take a look. (They aim the instruments at her.)*

Scene 4

Support group. Women drink from Styrofoam coffee cups. The scene should start realistically, in chairs, then move into a heightened, presentational staging, and then back to chairs.

JO. Hi my name is Jo.
GROUP. Hi Jo. *(Applause.)*
FIFI. Hi, my name is Fifi.
GROUP. Hi Fifi. *(Applause.)*
THERESA. I'm Theresa.
GROUP. Hi, Theresa. *(Applause.)*
THERESA. I didn't know 'til I was married.
JO. I thought my life was ruined.
FIFI. My life was over.
THERESA. I'd never really looked.
JO. It looked normal from the outside.
THERESA. My husband was surprised.
FIFI. I read about it in *Cosmo. (Holds up* Cosmopolitan *magazine.)*
JO. They wrote about it in *Cosmo. (Holds up* Cosmopolitan *magazine.)*
THERESA. We read about it in *Cosmo. (Holds up Cosmopolitan magazine.)*
GROUP. *(Reading from* Cosmo.*)* Sometimes nature slips up.
JO. Cleft palate —
THERESA. — harelip —
FIFI. — clubfoot —
JO. — but there is one abnormality few of us have heard of.

GROUP. Yet today, there are twenty to thirty thousand women, like us, in the U.S. alone who were born with: C.A.V.
THERESA. *(Not from* Cosmo.*)* I found out on my wedding night. We were in Bermuda. I was still a virgin.
FIFI. *(Not from* Cosmo.*)* I found out as a teenager. You know, on my own.
JO. *(Not from* Cosmo.*)* I found out at the doctor.
THERESA. My husband was unable to penetrate. Much to our displeasure.
FIFI. I knew right away something was wrong.
THERESA. For months I was still a virgin.
JO. I was having an examination. He called in his partners.
GROUP. We were diagnosed with C.A.V.
THERESA. Congenital —
FIFI. — absence —
JO. — of —
THERESA. — the —
GROUP. *(Loud whisper to Susie.)* — vagina.
THERESA. I became hysterical.
FIFI. I felt like I wasn't a woman.
JO. I was a freak.
THERESA. I had surgery as fast as possible. *(Overlapping section:)*
FIFI. *(Reads from* Cosmo.*)* Skin from the buttocks is wrapped around a mold, held in place by suturing. Fourteen days later the mold is removed.
JO. *(Reads.)* Nature, unfortunately, recognizing the opening as foreign, wants to close it down.
THERESA. *(Reads.)* A patient must keep it open with frequent coitus or by using dilators regularly. *(Overlapping ends.)*
GROUP. *(Reads.)* One day a doctor heard of a woman who created hers through coitus, and it didn't close down.
JO. He thought it would be possible —
FIFI. — to create a neo vagina without surgery —
THERESA. — and he began experimenting.
JO. He had a —
FIFI. — patient sit on —
THERESA. — a stool with —
JO. — a Lucite —
FIFI. — dilator for —
THERESA. — fifteen to —
JO. — thirty minutes —

FIFI. — a day.
JO. It —
THERESA. — involved —
FIFI. — time —
JO. — patience —
THERESA. — and —
FIFI. — motivation —
GROUP. — but it worked.
GROUP and SUSIE. Once C.A.V was a devastating diagnosis for any young girl. But today, women, like us, can lead satisfying, sexually active lives.
THERESA. I had the surgery. You have to keep it in use. My husband loves it.
FIFI. I used the stool.
JO. I had the surgery, then it closed, then I used the stool.
THERESA. I'm a changed woman.
JO. I stare at skyscrapers.
FIFI. My husband really loves me now.
THERESA. I like to keep objects inside of mine.
JO. I was afraid after my first one closed down.
THERESA. Spare change, my keys, date book. Things I don't want to misplace.
JO. My boyfriend was very supportive. He loves it.
FIFI. They love it.
GROUP. Your boyfriend will love it.

Scene 5

Phone call. Gary with money, a computer, calculator; wearing athletic/career clothes. Loud sounds of TV sports.

SUSIE. Gary, it's Susie.
GARY. Oh hi. *(He catches a football.)*
SUSIE. What are you doing?
GARY. *(He counts money.)* I'm keeping very busy with external activities so I don't have to experience any inner feelings.
SUSIE. Oh.

GARY. *(He works on a computer.)* You know sports, cars, sex, money, career advancement. I'm very busy, not much time to talk.
SUSIE. I see.
GARY. *(He watches a game on TV, yells at the set.)* Pass! Run! Jump! GO!
SUSIE. Well I just wanted to let you know I'm getting one.
GARY. Oh? *(He pulls out the TV remote. Silence.)*
SUSIE. It should be ready in a while. I think you'll love it. I'll be a virgin, Gary.
GARY. *(With reverence, he puts on a baseball cap. A baseball bat appears, he takes it.)* Give me the chance, I'll hit a home run.
SUSIE. Yeah?
GARY. Let me know when it's opening day. *(He swings the bat.)*

Scene 6

Doctor's waiting room. Sexy-looking women sit.

WOMAN 1. I'm having my breasts enlarged.
WOMAN 2. I'm having mine reduced.
WOMAN 4. I'm having my lips inflated.
WOMAN 3. I'm having my hips deflated.
WOMAN 4. Collagen injection.
WOMAN 2. Silicone rejection.
WOMAN 3. Nipple lift.
WOMAN 4. This is my fifth.
WOMAN 1. Chemical peel.
WOMAN 3. Cheeks revealed.
WOMAN 1. Liposuction.
WOMAN 2. Bulge reduction.
WOMAN 4. Ribs removed.
WOMAN 3. Jaw —
WOMAN 2. — reimproved *(All look at Susie.)*
SUSIE. *(Whispers.)* Vagina. *(Full voice.)* I'm getting a *(Whispers.)* vagina.
WOMAN 2. Really?
WOMAN 3. Wow.

WOMAN 4. A new one?
WOMAN 1. I never thought of that.

Scene 7

Phone call. Gary is drumming.

SUSIE. Hi, it's Susie. What are you doing?
GARY. Drumming. I read that classic "pumping iron in the john" book. *(He drums.)* My name is Gary, son of Barry.
SUSIE. I wanted to give you an update.
GARY. *(Stops drumming.)* I'm finding my manhood. If you're gonna talk about — about, I mean, women's parts and, eew you know eew.
SUSIE. Well, I'm in the middle of a session. I've been sitting here. Expanding. And, Gary, do you want to know what I think about?
GARY. What?
SUSIE. Sometimes I think about you. *(He turns to her.)* And, Gary. It's beginning to work.
GARY. It is? *(He drums with enthusiasm.)*

Scene 8

Support group.

SUSIE. It's beginning to work.
GROUP. How do you feel?
SUSIE. Different.

JO.	THERESA.	FIFI.
Yes?	I knew it.	I told you.

SUSIE. I have — I have this yearning feeling.

JO	THERESA	FIFI.
Oh yes, oh yes.	Oh really?	Tell us.

SUSIE. Like I need to nurture someone.
JO. Try volunteering.
SUSIE. And an interest in children.
FIFI. I bought a puppy.
SUSIE. And a need to relate to other relationships.
THERESA. Try the afternoon talk shows.
SUSIE. And at the same time I feel angry. I see, I see injustice and sexism and it makes me angry. It's confusing. Things are getting very confused.
FIFI. Oh, that.
JO. Being a woman.
THERESA. Try therapy.
JO. Oh, yes.
FIFI. Being a woman.
THERESA. Counseling.
JO. Oh, that.
FIFI. That.
GROUP. Oh, *that.*

Scene 9

Susie alone. Almost like a nursery rhyme.

SUSIE. The Freudian said penis envy. A Jungian, animus fear. Psychiatrist said chemical imbalance. Psychopharmacologist thought Prozac needed here. The psychic said the answer is the future; psychologist, the future's in the past, don't fear. Internist called a gynecologist, support group says — *(Support group appears.)*
GROUP. Just keep stretching it, dear! *(Group exits.)*

Scene 10

Susie, alone.

SUSIE. Oh my God. I have I have, this empty feeling. I feel so so, empty. I want to find fulfillment. I want to fill this empty feeling. I want to be pretty. I have to help others. I want to wear silk teddies and push-up bras. I want men to open the door for me and then I want to say, "Do I look like I have no arms?" I want to go dancing in high heels and let men lead, and then I get mad when they don't know the steps and I'm not supposed to show them. I want men to notice me and then I want to punch them when they stare. I want to feed children in the Third World and scream at the white male politicians who sent the guns there and screwed it up in the first place. I want men to give me a seat on the subway and I want to tell the one next to me to stop taking up so much room, why don't you close your legs, what have you got between them, an aircraft carrier?! I want to lash back at the backlash. I have a hole inside me now. All of this because of a hole?

Scene 11

Gary dials the phone. He takes a deflated blow-up doll out of a box. Susie picks up.

GARY. Susie.
SUSIE. Hi.
GARY. Listen, I'm I'm uh practicing for the big day, you know, exercises, technique, defining goals to make sure we achieve them, you know, win the gold medal, blue ribbon, first place, one for the Gipper.
SUSIE. Gary, you make me really angry.
GARY. Oh. *(He drops the doll.)*

SUSIE. I I want to hurt you.
GARY. Well, then, I I want to get away from you.
SUSIE. I wouldn't nurture you if you were the last human on earth.
GARY. I wouldn't get near you with a ten-foot pole.
SUSIE. Well your testicles are hairy!
GARY. And your vagina is — missing!
SUSIE. *(She talks directly to him.)* Not anymore.
GARY. *(He talks directly to her.)* It isn't?
SUSIE. No.
GARY. Can I come over?
SUSIE. I'm wearing crotchless panties.
GARY. I'll be right there. *(He exits.)*

Scene 12

Susie unbuttons her two top buttons and puts on lipstick. Gary enters wearing a test pilot hat.

SUSIE. Hi.
GARY. Hi, sexy. You ready?
SUSIE. What are you wearing?
GARY. Test pilot, ready for takeoff.
SUSIE. Gary, before we go any further, I just have to tell you —
GARY. Go where no man has gone before.
SUSIE. That I think you're a jerk.
GARY. Can I touch it now?
SUSIE. And a pig.
GARY. Oink oink. Now can I?
SUSIE. The way you dumped me then and the way you want me now.
GARY. Come on, baby, let's go exploring.
SUSIE. All because of a hole.
GARY. I want to be your Christopher Columbus.
SUSIE. Gary.
GARY. Cortez, Ponce De Leon. Neil Armstrong. *(He puts on goggles.)*
SUSIE. That does it. I changed my mind.
GARY. What?

SUSIE. I'm not interested, I'm just not interested. It's my vagina. It is. I made it, it's mine — V-A-G-I-N-A. I don't have to share. I can have a satisfying life without sharing it with you. So, no. It's my hole. And if I want to spend my life crawled up inside of it without you or anyone, then I will. And if you don't like it, you can go. If that's all you're here for, leave. Find yourself another hole.

GARY. *(Stunned. Looks at her, confused.)* Well. What about your mouth?

SUSIE. Well, what about the inside of one of your drums? Or why don't you hollow out your baseball bat? I know, just unzip your pants and head for the Holland Tunnel. Even better, Gary, use your own hole, the one between your ears, just put your dick in your head and fuck what little you have of your own brains out!

GARY. *(Beat.)* Nice. I'm really glad you've found yourself.

SUSIE. Me too. *(Pause. They stand there.)* So, what are you waiting for? Leave. I'm not the only hole in the universe.

GARY. *(Pause.)* I don't want to leave.

SUSIE. Why not?

GARY. I don't know.

SUSIE. Why did you ever even talk to me in the first place?

GARY. Mmm. Your face. I think. Something about your face. Made me want to say hi. And then, something about what you said.

SUSIE. What did I say?

GARY. Hi. But it was the way you said it. "Hi." And when I asked if I could see you sometime and you said, "That would be nice," that was nice. I guess I liked you. And, well, I guess I kinda like you feisty even better.

SUSIE. Oh.

GARY. Why did you talk to me?

SUSIE. You had nice buns.

GARY. Yeah?

SUSIE. *(She shrugs.)* I looked at you and I knew I wanted — to wrestle.

GARY. *(Beat.)* Susie. I know I can be a jerk. I couldn't — I didn't know how to — I. Sorry. Look, what if we — what if we just, you know, tried to be, like, close.

SUSIE. What do you mean?

GARY. You know, like, lie down and do the close thing.

SUSIE. What?

GARY. You know, that talking and feeling thing. How would that be?

SUSIE. I don't know.

GARY. Yeah, forget it.
SUSIE. *(Beat.)* It might be OK.
GARY. Yeah?
SUSIE. Yeah.
GARY. We could try.
SUSIE. We could. Take off the helmet. *(He does. Music plays. They take off their shoes as the Ensemble enters with sheet and pillows to create a vertical bed. They "get in bed," on opposite ends. They, very gingerly and slowly, get close. They sigh. They smile.)*
GARY. So, how is it?
SUSIE. It's — nice. How is it for you?
GARY. Nice.
SUSIE. Gary?
GARY. Yeah?
SUSIE. Do you sit on the subway with your legs spread?
GARY. Yeah.
SUSIE. Why?
GARY. Just born that way, I guess.
SUSIE. Oh.
GARY. I think I'm gonna fall asleep now. Good night.
SUSIE. 'Night. *(He snores loudly, then pushes her all the way to the edge of the bed.)* Gary?
GARY. *(Asleep.)* Huh?
SUSIE. *(With clarity.)* Move over. *(He rolls over to his edge. They are apart. Susie reaches out her hand across the bed, Gary reaches out his hand. They touch. Blackout.)*

End of Play

PROPERTY LIST

Paper (DOCTOR CHECKUP)
Phones (GARY and SUSIE)
Screwdriver (GARY)
Medical examining instruments (DOCTORS)
Styrofoam coffee cups (JO, FIFI, THERESA, SUSIE)
Cosmopolitan magazine (FIFI, JO, THERESA)
Money (GARY)
Computer (GARY)
Calculator (GARY)
Football (STAGE MANAGER) [thrown from offstage]
TV remote control (GARY)
Baseball cap (GARY)
Baseball bat (STAGE MANAGER)
Drum (GARY)
Blow-up doll (GARY)
Lipstick (SUSIE)
Goggles (GARY)
Sheets (ENSEMBLE)
Pillows (ENSEMBLE)

SOUND EFFECTS

TV sports
Music

DEAR KENNETH BLAKE

DEAR KENNETH BLAKE was first produced by Ensemble Studio Theatre in New York City (Curt Dempster, Artistic Director) in their 1994 Marathon. It was directed by Brian Mertes. The cast was as follows:

TINA .... Jodi Long
KENNETH .... Matthew Cowles

DEAR KENNETH BLAKE was produced in Los Angeles in 1997 at Theatre Geo, directed by Geo Hartley. It received a Drama-Logue Award in Playwriting. The cast was as follows:

TINA .... Susan Fukuda
KENNETH .... James Lurie

CHARACTERS

TINA, 30s. From Cambodia. She has great dignity and strength. She has a sense of humor, and knows how to be blunt. She wears a blouse and a skirt.

KENNETH, 40s. He has great dignity and strength. Gruff. Blunt. Used to solitude. He wears work clothes and work boots, no socks.

PLACE

The apartment where Tina works and the farm where Kenneth works.

TIME

Late spring. 1994.

DEAR KENNETH BLAKE

Scene 1

Two separate areas. Tina is in the apartment where she works. She sits behind a window box that rests on a small bench, a watering can beside her. Kenneth is on the farm where he works. He stands behind a makeshift barbed wire fence he is building. He talks to an unseen person.

TINA. Dear Kenneth Blake, I saw you this afternoon on the television talk show, and I want to say I wish you best of luck in your new home. You seem like a nice man.
KENNETH. If this is the best I can do then this is the best I can do, but I tell you I'm not sleeping with that bunch of beggars and drug addicts!
TINA. *(She starts to make small holes in the soil.)* I hope you stop drinking and smoking, and learn to breathe fresh air and have a new start.
KENNETH. *(He starts cutting "barbs" out of a wire hanger.)* Telling me when to sleep and how to comb my hair and wash my asshole, and when to snore, and who the hell are they, huh? Bunch of panhandlers trying to steal my cigareets?
TINA. You say you are looking to meet a wife in the country and maybe a pretty one with blonde hair.
KENNETH. Well, I never begged for nothin' in my whole life, you hear?
TINA. Maybe we can write letters and be friends.
KENNETH. And I'll tell you another thing, I'm not a slave, and the only time anyone ever wants something from me around here is when they want something from me!
TINA. Dear Kenneth Blake, I hope you are doing well. I did not hear from you, and I wonder if you got my last letter.

KENNETH. You expect me to get up at the crack of dawn after sleeping with this bunch of losers and work all day, and pay me next to nothin' —

TINA. Maybe you did not. I hope you are learning to plant, and getting along with the other people that have no homes and are also learning to plant. Have you met any nice friends?

KENNETH. — to grow these organic damn vegetables, like they're a religion 'cause they have no damn chemicals on them —

TINA. *(She puts seeds into the soil.)* Dear Kenneth Blake,

KENNETH. — and you charge a fortune of money by selling 'em to a bunch of long hairs and yuppies who pay quintuple price for 'em 'cause they don't want any toxins in their food —

TINA. My letters don't get returned, so I hope you are reading them, and are too busy to write.

KENNETH. — while they go out into the street and breathe in more toxins than could fit on all the organic tomatoes they could eat in twenty years. And you do all this 'cause you say you have a pact with Mother Earth.

TINA. In the house where I work they have a terrace with plants and flowers, and I think about you. I watched you on that show while I ironed, and was sad you had to live in a train tunnel for so many years, and then they made you leave. When I was a girl we had a house, and they made us leave. I am glad they have a good program to teach you to be a farmer.

KENNETH. And now you tell me I can't keep my pet rabbit in the damn "communal sleeping room" 'cause those stinky bums don't like the smell?! 'Cause I won't give the rabbit a shower!?

TINA. How does your rabbit like it there?

KENNETH. Well, I ain't gonna just dump her! Where I goes, she goes!

TINA. P.S. When I saw your face I think you have a look in your eyes I understand.

KENNETH. I would leave here if I could, but I can't 'cause you don't pay enough money. Even Mr. Greenjeans made enough money!

TINA. Dear Kenneth Blake, Do you like being on a farm? Do you work too hard maybe?

KENNETH. I got nowhere to go and no way to get there.

TINA. Do your eyes look different now that you live in the country? Is it hard to get along with people after being alone for so long? Is it different to have a home after not having one?

KENNETH. Working like a dog for a do-good-for-the-homeless organic hippie —
TINA. Do you wish you had a family? Have you found a wife?
KENNETH. — think you take a bunch of drug addict drunks and put 'em on a farm —
TINA. *(She waters the soil.)* Is it lonely to be in a far away place?
KENNETH. — and they'll turn into a do-good organic hippie like you.
TINA. I think about your face, and I wonder if you wonder about me. Maybe we will never meet, but at least there is someone who knows how I feel.
KENNETH. I may not be able to leave here, but me and my rabbit will not sleep with those smelly animal-hating bums! You say you got a pact with Mother Earth, well she gave birth to my rabbit, and she don't mind the smell!
TINA. Dear Kenneth Blake, You have a look in your eyes I know. *(Pause, as they both change their focus.)*
KENNETH. Dear Tina, Uh. Thanks for your letters. Things here stink. I don't know how to keep doing this, and I don't know what else to do. They got me planting these guru tomatoes all day. My feet are so tired they're gonna drop off. Keep writing, if you like. It's nice to get to know you. They want me to give up my rabbit, and I won't. Maybe someday we could meet.
TINA. Kenneth, Kenneth, Kenneth, we can. *(Scene transition. Lights dim. Music.)*

Scene 2

Lights up. Kenneth is working on the barbed wire fence. Tina enters, carrying a tote bag. She carefully looks to see if it is him. He doesn't see her.

TINA. Kenneth.
KENNETH. *(He doesn't look up.)* Yeah?
TINA. Tina Sen.
KENNETH. *(Gruff.)* Your what?
TINA. Tina Sen.

KENNETH. *(He looks at her, He stands.)* Oh.
TINA. You remember?
KENNETH. Uh.
TINA. I come to see with you.
KENNETH. What?
TINA. I come to see you.
KENNETH. Oh. Well, uh. I'm, uh, not much to look at and —
TINA. You said maybe we could meet, and I thought maybe we could. I brought you some shoes for your feet and some food for the rabbit.
KENNETH. You work for a charity, is that it? Some kind of pen pal United Way? Well, I don't take no charity.
TINA. No. From me. A present from me.
KENNETH. Huh?
TINA. A gift. Like, uh, birthday.
KENNETH. Oh. Well, you got the wrong guy, I ain't got no birthday. *(He crosses away from her to his toolbox. She takes a new pair of shoes out of her bag, puts them on the ground.)*
TINA. See?
KENNETH. Look, uh, I, uh, don't know what to say.
TINA. You can say thank you.
KENNETH. Yeah, right. Thank you.
TINA. And you can say, "Please, let's talk," or you say, "I don't wish to see you," and I can go.
KENNETH. Now, now, how — how did you get here?
TINA. I walked.
KENNETH. You walked all the way from New York?
TINA. No. I take the bus.
KENNETH. And from the bus stop you —
TINA. — Walked.
KENNETH. How long it take you?
TINA. Ten hours.
KENNETH. Jesus. I. Look, um, I'm a little, I mean, what made you come here, I, uh, don't imagine you were just in the neighborhood, I mean you didn't just come to get some fresh organic air.
TINA. No.
KENNETH. No.
TINA. Kenneth.
KENNETH. Listen, I'm uh. I'm doing something here. And it's important. I mean. I wrote you that — but. I didn't. You shouldn't. See. I'm … busy. *(He crosses to the window box.)*

TINA. I give myself to you, and I wonder if you give yourself to me.
KENNETH. What?
TINA. There is no one to choose for me, and I saw you and you say you wanted a wife, and I want to be your wife, but I don't have blonde hair.
KENNETH. What?
TINA. If you want me. Do you think you might want me?
KENNETH. Well, I mean —
TINA. I would be a good wife.
KENNETH. Well, we just, we just don't do it like that, I mean, you don't just take a bus and, that's not how we do it, maybe that's how you do it from — where are you from?
TINA. Cambodia.
KENNETH. Well, that's very far from here, and this isn't. I mean, we take our time here.
TINA. How old are you?
KENNETH. Forty-five.
TINA. That's time enough, don't you think?
KENNETH. Well, well, I uh — what about your mother and your —
TINA. Dead.
KENNETH. *(He picks up window box, crosses back to the fence, puts it down.)* Well, I'm sorry, but that still —
TINA. At home it would be different. I would never be so bold. I would always be modest, but this is America, and they say on the talk show if a horse gallops by your house you must jump on or it will gallop by without you.
KENNETH. What?
TINA. Maybe we can go inside to your house and talk more.
KENNETH. This is my house.
TINA. *(She looks around.)* This?
KENNETH. This is where I sleep.
TINA. Outside?
KENNETH. It's a lot better than with those creeps, and I can keep Bugs with me. Suits me fine. I don't need much. Plenty of fresh air out here.
TINA. Oh.
KENNETH. You wouldn't believe some of the things that go on around here. You just wouldn't believe it.
TINA. I would believe.
KENNETH. Well, I guess that's it. Maybe you were looking for a

nice home in the country, I mean, maybe that's what this was. Well, I ain't got that, and I ain't got a white picket fence or a dog named Spot, and there ain't no galloping horses around here, just me and a rabbit, and a barbed wire fence to keep out the creeps, so I'm not your ticket to a better life. I guess you can get the next bus.

TINA. *(She leans over the fence to him.)* It's private here?

KENNETH. Believe me, no one comes out to where I am. Popular, I ain't, and I guess you can see why. *(She puts her scarf on the ground, and sits.)* What are you doing?

TINA. I think that you sit down now, and we sit here together in your house … Your feet hurt?

KENNETH. Does a rabbit shit on a farm? … Yeah.

TINA. Then you sit here, and maybe we eat something for lunch and —

KENNETH. Boy oh boy, I don't, I mean, I don't, what you just, who said you could —

TINA. If your feet hurt, it's good to sit and take off your shoes.

KENNETH. Well —

TINA. I see you don't want to. You think what is this crazy — a crazy lady — why would I do that? I am afraid of this crazy lady I do not even know. But what can be bad, huh? What is there for you to lose? You don't have to want to get married. I am just asking you to come here, and we say words to each other, and we see which words come out. *(He is looking away.)* I see you look around. Sometimes you can look around so much you don't see what's next to you. *(He almost looks at her.)* I see you almost look at me. You can look at me. I understand hurting feet.

KENNETH. Oh yeah?

TINA. Yeah. You ask why I came here, well, I learn that life is short, and in this country you have to go for it, or it's gone. But first you have to sit, and you have to take off your shoes, and then we see.

KENNETH. Lady, if I sit next to you and take off these shoes, you'll want to get away so fast you won't need a bus to get to New York. I mean, they stink. I mean, we're talking about stink.

TINA. I decide that.

KENNETH. My feet, well, see my feet are like a hot foot, you know what that is? It's like on a cartoon, you ever see that? They put a match on your feet and it burns, and I got one on each toe that won't go out and, well, it's kinda like rotting burning foot flesh. Not too nice. So, I don't think so. *(He crosses to the toolbox.)*

TINA. *(She takes handfuls of dirt from the window box, and puts them*

on the ground.) Maybe if you put them in the ground, it's cooler.
KENNETH. No amount of organic dirt is gonna help me.
TINA. Maybe not, but you do it anyway.
KENNETH. Oh?
TINA. Maybe if we think things aren't going to work sometimes we do it anyway. Maybe we are just afraid. Maybe we think it cannot be different. You say Cambodia is far from here, but they write about it in the New York *Times*. And do you know what they write about now? They had elections this year. And this country is trying to help make peace there. How do they think they can do that — now? How can they think they can do that? *(He looks at her.)* I lose my family, my home, my country. I come here and see a man on TV, and he has the eyes of my father when they took him away. I watch him, and I feel a love for this man, this man I don't know, this man I am afraid will think I'm crazy if I tell him. I write him many letters, he writes me one back, I take a bus and I find him, and I see he does have those eyes, and I see — I can see — he has a soul like my family, and he doesn't smile when he looks at me, and he does not want the gifts I bring him, and he says he has no home, and I am afraid, and I do it anyway. I ask him to take off his shoes, and when he says "no" I am again afraid, and I think it will not work, but I know, I know what I see, even if he doesn't, even if he will never know, I know, and I say, Dear Kenneth Blake, I say it anyway, if your feet hurt you take off your shoes and put them in the dirt. I ask for nothing else. Just that. *(He crosses to her, sits, and takes off his shoes. He puts his feet in the dirt. He feels relief as his feet feel better.)*
KENNETH. I'm not talking about marrying you, I'm just — I'm not good at talking. I don't get along with people when I talk. How about you? How about your feet?
TINA. No. My eyes. My eyes.
KENNETH. What?
TINA. They cry and sometimes I can barely see. Look, see they cry.
KENNETH. Oh.
TINA. Look, I cry. *(She laughs.)* Even if I am happy, I cry.
KENNETH. Oh … Tina. *(She wipes the tears from her eyes, then drips them onto the dirt covering his feet.)*
TINA. My tears water your feet.
KENNETH. Yeah. Huh.
TINA. Is it OK if we just sit here? We just sit here in your house. I like your house.

KENNETH. Uh, sure.
TINA. I like the view. And the furniture.
KENNETH. Sure …
TINA. I've come a long way to get to your house.
KENNETH. Uh huh.
TINA. I brought food.
KENNETH. Oh.
TINA. We can sit here. My tears drip onto your feet and we can see what will grow. *(They sit. She leans over to cry onto the dirt that covers his feet.)*

End of Play

PROPERTY LIST

Window box and soil (TINA)
Wire cutter (KENNETH)
Hanger (KENNETH)
Seeds (TINA)
Watering can (TINA)
Tote bag containing a pair of shoes (TINA)
Scarf (TINA)

SOUND EFFECTS

Music

NEW PLAYS

★ **INTIMATE APPAREL by Lynn Nottage.** The moving and lyrical story of a turn-of-the-century black seamstress whose gifted hands and sewing machine are the tools she uses to fashion her dreams from the whole cloth of her life's experiences. "…Nottage's play has a delicacy and eloquence that seem absolutely right for the time she is depicting…" *–NY Daily News.* "…thoughtful, affecting…The play offers poignant commentary on an era when the cut and color of one's dress—and of course, skin—determined whom one could and could not marry, sleep with, even talk to in public." *–Variety.* [2M, 4W] ISBN: 0-8222-2009-1

★ **BROOKLYN BOY by Donald Margulies.** A witty and insightful look at what happens to a writer when his novel hits the bestseller list. "The characters are beautifully drawn, the dialogue sparkles…" *–nytheatre.com.* "Few playwrights have the mastery to smartly investigate so much through a laugh-out-loud comedy that combines the vintage subject matter of successful writer-returning-to-ethnic-roots with the familiar mid-life crisis." *–Show Business Weekly.* [4M, 3W] ISBN: 0-8222-2074-1

★ **CROWNS by Regina Taylor.** Hats become a springboard for an exploration of black history and identity in this celebratory musical play. "Taylor pulls off a Hat Trick: She scores thrice, turning CROWNS into an artful amalgamation of oral history, fashion show, and musical theater…" *–TheatreMania.com.* "…wholly theatrical…Ms. Taylor has created a show that seems to arise out of spontaneous combustion, as if a bevy of department-store customers simultaneously decided to stage a revival meeting in the changing room." *–NY Times.* [1M, 6W (2 musicians)] ISBN: 0-8222-1963-8

★ **EXITS AND ENTRANCES by Athol Fugard.** The story of a relationship between a young playwright on the threshold of his career and an aging actor who has reached the end of his. "[Fugard] can say more with a single line than most playwrights convey in an entire script…Paraphrasing the title, it's safe to say this drama, making its memorable entrance into our consciousness, is unlikely to exit as long as a theater exists for exceptional work." *–Variety.* "A thought-provoking, elegant and engrossing new play…" *–Hollywood Reporter.* [2M] ISBN: 0-8222-2041-5

★ **BUG by Tracy Letts.** A thriller featuring a pair of star-crossed lovers in an Oklahoma City motel facing a bug invasion, paranoia, conspiracy theories and twisted psychological motives. "…obscenely exciting…top-flight craftsmanship. Buckle up and brace yourself…" *–NY Times.* "…[a] thoroughly outrageous and thoroughly entertaining play…the possibility of enemies, real and imagined, to squash has never been more theatrical." *–A.P.* [3M, 2W] ISBN: 0-8222-2016-4

★ **THOM PAIN (BASED ON NOTHING) by Will Eno.** An ordinary man muses on childhood, yearning, disappointment and loss, as he draws the audience into his last-ditch plea for empathy and enlightenment. "It's one of those treasured nights in the theater—treasured nights anywhere, for that matter—that can leave you both breathless with exhilaration and…in a puddle of tears." *–NY Times.* "Eno's words…are familiar, but proffered in a way that is constantly contradictory to our expectations. Beckett is certainly among his literary ancestors." *–nytheatre.com.* [1M] ISBN: 0-8222-2076-8

★ **THE LONG CHRISTMAS RIDE HOME by Paula Vogel.** Past, present and future collide on a snowy Christmas Eve for a troubled family of five. "…[a] lovely and hauntingly original family drama…a work that breathes so much life into the theater." *–Time Out.* "…[a] delicate visual feast…" *–NY Times.* "…brutal and lovely…the overall effect is magical." *–NY Newsday.* [3M, 3W] ISBN: 0-8222-2003-2